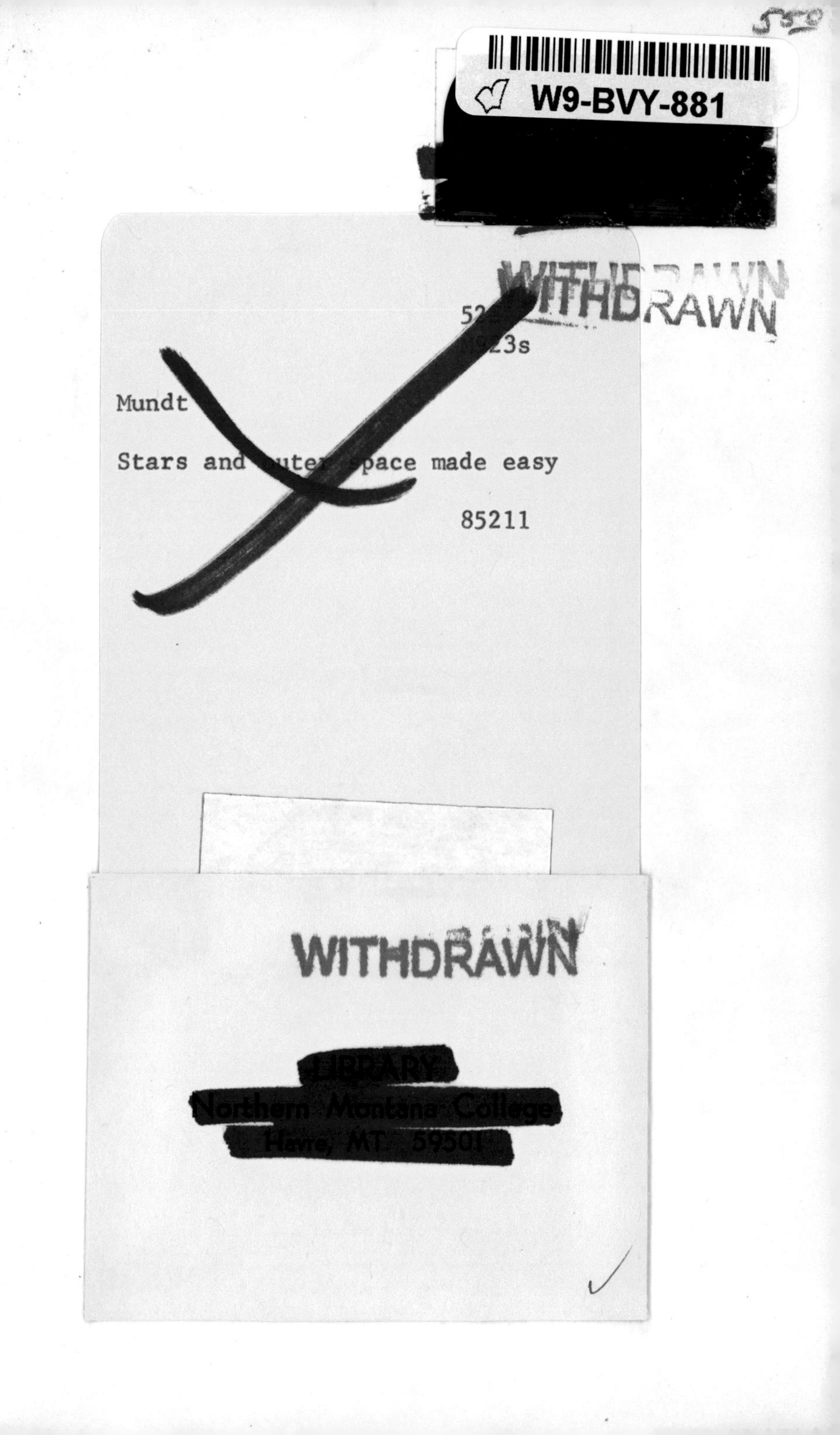
W9-BVY-881
WITHDRAWN
52
M923s
Mundt
Stars and outer space made easy
85211
WITHDRAWN
LIBRARY
Northern Montana College
Havre, MT 59501

Stars & Outer Space made easy

Revised Edition

FRONTISPIECE:

STAR CLOUDS in AQUILA and SAGITTARIUS. Photograph courtesy of Lick Observatory.

Stars & Outer Space made easy

Revised Edition

By Carlos S Mundt

Emeritus Professor of Astronomy and
Mathematics, San Francisco State College

edited by Vinson Brown

85211

Naturegraph Publishers, Healdsburg, California 95448.

ACKNOWLEDGMENTS

Grateful acknowledgments and thanks of the author are extended to the following:

To the University of Chicago Press for permission to reproduce figure 2; to Dr. Charles J. Krieger for the preparation of the Star Maps; to the editors of "Sky and Telescope" for their kind permission to reproduce figure 3; to the staff of the Lick Observatory for the selection and reproduction of the many plates and figures; to the staff of the Hale Observatories for the permission to use four of their photographic reproductions; and especially to the many friendly teachers and student observers, who have pointed out the needs the beginner, and have given warm encouragement.

523
M923s

Library of Congress Cataloging in Publication Data

Mundt, Carlos S

Stars and Outer Space Made Easy.

Bibliography: p.

1. Astronomy—Observers' manuals. I. Title.

QB63.M76 1974 523 74-6491

Copyright © by Carlos S Mundt 1963
Copyright © by Carlos S Mundt 1974

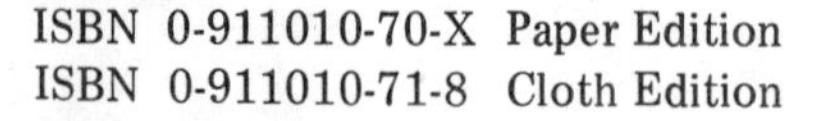

ISBN 0-911010-70-X Paper Edition
ISBN 0-911010-71-8 Cloth Edition

Naturegraph Publishers, Inc., Healdsburg, California 95448.

BoT

TABLE OF CONTENTS

5.06

7-24-75

FOREWORD

The progress of astronomy during the recent decade has been nothing short of astonishing and this has meant the appearance of a veritable deluge of books dealing with various phases of the subject. Unfortunately, a disappointingly small number have been written with the interested but uninformed layman in mind. Hence, no apology is needed for the present volume, since a teaching experience of several decades on the secondary, college, adult education and television levels has indicated a need for a book in which simplicity would be the keynote and complete self-use would become basic. The task of selection of recent material has been quite difficult, but has been achieved by continually keeping in mind the minimum requirements of the newcomer to this field.

Novato, California

Carlos S Mundt

Chapter I
THE STARS

Introduction

So you want to know the stars. You want to be able to locate those same stars which have served as guides to navigators from time immemorial. Magellan, Captain Cook, Lindbergh, Byrd, and the navigators in the giant airliners that are, at this moment, winging their way over the four quarters of the globe—all have used these stars. From the lowliest tramp steamer to the sleekest ocean greyhound, the navigators have charted their course by the stars. Ancient scientists spent much time in studying the riddle of the stars and modern scientists continue that study. The recognition of the groups of stars which we call "constellations" is ancient, indeed; the origins of some go so far back that they cannot be completely traced.

Knowing the stars and constellations always has been basic to the practice of navigation, while to the layman there is a fascination in their study which cannot be described. To the scientist, the navigator, and the average individual alike a knowledge of the heavens is of interest, since the stars are always with us, no matter in what part of the globe we live. In knowing something about these twinkling points of light we obtain a closer relationship to the past and a great appreciation of the marvels of the physical world. Besides, it is an accomplishment of which one may well be proud, to be able to recognize old friends among the hosts of stars from one year to the next.

The beginner is often slowed or completely discouraged in undertaking the task of knowing the heavens, even in an elementary fashion. This is partly because of the seeming impossibility of the task before him, but is often because of the difficulties in "getting started". In other words, the desire is already at hand, but the actual practice proves so difficult that it almost always ends in failure. The blame for this must be divided between the beginner himself, whose stock of patience is not always equal to his task, and the writers of introductory books and manuals. Too often these writers seem to be unable to place themselves in the position of the beginner, who may wish to be self-taught. Too often the principles and their various applications are presented in such a complicated manner, that the beginner finds the material far beyond his depth because of the great complexity and technicality which he encounters.

Here we will attempt to overcome these difficulties in two ways: (a) all technical matters are reduced to a minimum; (b) all instructions are given in as simple a manner as possible. When certain technicalities are omitted, this is deliberately done, since their inclusion would often be inconsistent with the general purpose of the book. Simplicity is the keynote throughout and is an objective to be kept in mind as we proceed.

CONSTELLATIONS

Astronomy is without doubt the oldest of the physical sciences. It was the first to indicate to man the existence of law in nature and its gradual development has unfolded horizons so broad and far-reaching as to be most breathtaking. In turn, the forward march of astronomical knowledge has been directed away from the earth, the sun and solar system to the vistas of millions of stars, an immense stellar system and even beyond it to the many exterior stellar systems.

For purposes of reference all ancient peoples have organized the starry heavens into groups of stars called constellations. We may simply define a constellation as a certain star grouping bearing a definite name for reference purposes. Very often such a constellation seems to show little resemblance to the animal, bird, fish or deity it was intended to represent, but this is the result of an extensive mythology, coupled with a lively imagination. Many constellations are thousands of years old and research indicates a striking similarity among some of them as pictured by different civilizations.

The earliest list of stars of which we have information was that gathered by Hipparchus, a Greek astronomer, at about 120 B.C. His catalog, containing 1000 stars, was further edited by Ptolemy of Alexandria (2nd century A.D.), who recognized 48 separate constellations. Of course, he included only those portions of the heavens which were visible from the Mediterranean regions.

After the voyages to the southern hemisphere had shown the existence of many more stars than had been known to the Greek world, attempts were made to continue the scheme by the creation of additional constellations, a number being based upon national achievements. This obviously created considerable confusion, but it was eventually overcome by an international agreement. We now recognize 88 distinct constellations and their specific abbreviations were adopted in 1922 by the International Astronomical Union (see listing of constellations and their abbreviations on page 52).

Mention should be made of a certain series of constellations which constitute a sort of belt called the "Zodiac", within which the Sun, Moon and the planets may always be found. These zodiacal constellations are called Aries (the ram), Taurus (the bull), Gemini (the twins), Cancer (the crab), Leo (the lion), Virgo (the virgin), Libra (the scales), Scorpio (the scorpion), Sagittarius (the archer), Capricornus (the goat), Aquarius (the water carrier), and Pisces (the fishes). These were known to the Greeks over 2000 years ago, but were not essentially Greek. They had come to the Greeks from still earlier civilizations in the Euphrates Valley in Asia Minor over 3000 years in the past.

The reader may well inquire if a knowledge of constellations is necessary. The answer is definitely "yes", but we may hasten to add this word of caution: no one can master the study of the heavens in one night! Care and deliberation and patience will pay well in the long run. "Rome was not built in a day", nor can one learn the entire heavens without some consistent effort. With much patience, and determination, though with a leisurely approach and a constant wish to learn, success will finally be achieved! Let us now investigate how this may be done.

ORIENTATION

In order to make our beginning in the art of "star gazing" we must first orient ourselves; in other words, we must have some knowledge of the four cardinal or main points of the compass as we prepare to look out into all the starlit skies. The best way to do this is to find north, which is easily accomplished by one of the following methods, to be undertaken in advance of the first evening of observation:

(1) Note the direction of the shadows in the vicinity of your observing place at noon; they will point northward. In this connection a flagpole, tree, or even a stick driven into the ground will furnish the best results.

(2) Visit the office of the city or county surveyor. He will be glad to show you a large scale map upon which the orientation of your own property is indicated. Should you have difficulty in reading the map he will help you.

(3) The scout trick of using your watch as a compass will enable you to do a fairly accurate job of orienting yourself at any time of day. Simply hold your watch flat with the face up and point the hour hand at the Sun; then mark half way between the hour and twelve, which will be SOUTH; opposite this, naturally, is NORTH.

(4) Should a noon observation prove inconvenient, then note the direction of the setting sun at evening. Face that direction and north will be at your right hand.

This initial step of orientation is of the greatest importance. Your entire success or failure will depend upon the determination of north at the place where you expect to do your observing (your backyard, your front porch, the top of a neighboring hill, etc.). It might be wise to determine north by more than one of the foregoing methods, so as to have a check on your work.

FIRST STEPS

Let us now suppose you have determined the direction of north and we are ready to make a start in actual observing. Select a clear, moonless night. Use a pocket flashlight which has been covered with a piece of ordinary tissue paper, secured with a rubber band. This makes it possible to go from the charts to the sky and vice versa without glare and eye discomfort. Always begin your observations at about 8:30 p.m. standard time.

Face NORTH. Turn to the circumpolar star map (no. 1 on page 44). Circumpolar means those constellations around the North Pole of the heavens. On the map you will find a number of underlined dates. Choose the nearest one to your date of observation and hold the chart so that the date is down, or in lowest position, as you hold the map in your hand.

If you proceed as outlined above, the entire northern heavens will appear as seen on the map you hold in your hand and you may immediately pick out one or both of the two most prominent constellations. These are Ursa Major (see page 51: Great Bear or "Big Dipper", as the seven main stars of this constellation are commonly called), and Cassiopeia (Chained Lady or Queen Cassiopeia, a W-shaped group of five stars). Now draw an imaginary line through the two stars in Ursa Major that are farthest from the Great Dipper handle. They are often called "the pointers". Extend this line about five times its length outward in a direction that water would "pour" out of the Dipper. You will now reach the North Star (Polaris), by following this line. This star is not of great brilliance, contrary to popular belief, but is really quite conspicuous since there are few other stars of nearly equal brightness nearby. It is the end star in the handle of Ursa Minor (Little Bear or "Little Dipper"). Note that the Little Dipper is upside down with respect to the Big Dipper and also that it occupies a much smaller area in the sky. The elevation of Polaris (the North Star) above your horizon approximates your latitude north of the equator in degrees.

Before proceeding to the use of other maps, make sure that you have mastered the entire northern (circumpolar) regions. Besides Ursa Major, Ursa Minor, and Cassiopeia, one should also be familiar with Draco (the Dragon) and Cepheus (the King). These last are not so easily found, since they do not contain very bright stars. Considerable moonlight or local lighting may make it quite impossible to locate them more than generally.

Note that, as time passes, the stars lying to the west (left) of the Pole Star will gradually drop lower, and those on the east (right) will gradually climb higher. This will be true during the several hours of observation on any given night, due to the Earth's rotation. It will also be true at a given observation hour through the year, which is the reason for the dates placed around the map. However, should an observation be made on a certain date and at a certain time, then the general aspect of the heavens will be repeated year after year at this same date and time.

The foregoing instructions should enable anyone possessing ordinary care and patience to become familiar with the chief constellations of the northern heavens after a few nights of trial, but much depends upon careful orientation and the determination of the scale of the sky against that of the map. Having located these northern constellations and impressed their geometrical shapes upon one's mind, the rest follows with ease. We will use these "northers" as our "markers" and go on to the use of the other maps.

Considerable moonlight will seriously dim all stars and of course it must follow that the dark of the Moon would be the best time for observing. Nearby artificial lighting will also make for difficulty, from which we may immediately conclude that the heart of a great city would not be a very satisfactory place for star study. Desert and mountain regions, being removed from city lights and smoke, usually prove best.

SOUTHERN SKIES

Other sky maps are provided so that the beginner may become acquainted with the remainder of the starry heavens. The simple expedient of focusing his attention on the south is employed. Each of the maps presents that portion of the heavens which is easily located at a particular time of the year if one makes a complete "about face" from his northern direction. All maps bear dates and times for their use.

Choose the proper map by the month of the year and face SOUTH, holding the book so that the bottom of the map is below. That portion of the map that extends from the bottom up to the point marked OVER X HEAD should lie directly before you. Note carefully the geometrical outlines of new constellations, such as triangles, squares, rectangles, etc. These are a great help in making positive identifications. Note also the sky area covered by various groups. This is often of great assistance, since the observer thus knows approximately how large a piece of sky is to be sought and will not be deceived by other chance groups that happen to look like the one he seeks.

For convenience the maps are continued from the point overhead into the northern constellations. This is to permit the use of the "marker" constellations previously learned and to show their position relationship to the southern part of the sky under study.

As the evening passes, the stars lying to the west (your right as you face south) will gradually drop lower, while those to the east (left) will gradually climb higher. This will also be true over a period of some months at the same observing time and is the reason for the date and time legends on each of the maps. All south sky maps are drawn for the middle latitudes of the United States. Use carefully and constantly to locate all constellations.

The interested student of the skies, as he becomes more and more acquainted with the constellations, will no doubt wonder as to their relative extent upon the celestial sphere. They range in size from very small groupings, such as Delphinus (the Dolphin) and Sagitta (the Arrow), to the very large ones, such as Ursa Major (the Great Bear) and Orion (the Hunter). It may prove useful to confine one's attention to the larger constellations at first and afterward gradually "fill in" the smaller and less conspicuous ones. The very dim and small constellations are listed on page 53 for reference sake only since they would, at this stage, be only confusing on our charts and in our discussion of the sky.

THE STARS

Various estimates have been made as to the total number of stars in the entire sky which are visible to the unaided eye at any one time. Much depends upon the locality of observation, since a restricted sky area, such as a canyon in a mountainous region, will cut down the total. The relative clearness of the atmosphere also has a very considerable effect. Under average conditions the figure of one thousand stars will be a fair and conservative estimate. This must be doubled of course if an observer were to study the skies before sunrise as well as those in the evening. It must be doubled again to include those visible in the southern hemisphere.

Mention has been made of the effect of the Earth's rotation on the visible heavens, the stars of the eastern skies gradually climbing higher, those of the western skies dropping down, while those in the vicinity of the Pole describe circles about it. A simple and very interesting experiment, which provides a permanent record for the amateur may be described as follows:

Any ordinary camera may be used as a star camera. It is only necessary to mount it temporarily in some fixed location, open the shutter, expose the film for the desired time, close the shutter, and then complete the developing and printing process. Obviously, familiarity with the mechanism of the shutter will be necessary in order to assure success. Most present day cameras are provided with a time exposure arrangement, so that the shutter may be opened with one operation and closed afterward with another. No special film is necessary, but special precautions need to be taken.

First of all, the camera must be placed on a rigid support. A box, a fence post, a window sill, or even better a cement structure will prove adequate. The camera need not be fastened down, although some means must be provided to prevent vibration of any kind. In setting up the camera for eastern or western sky exposure, it is only necessary to point it in the desired direction. For the northern (polar) exposure, it is necessary to "sight" over the top of the camera and probably raise the front slightly by a small block of wood, the final result being similar to Plate 1, although each star circle will be curtailed according to the length of exposure. Six hours exposure is most satisfactory.

One very important word of caution: nearby lighting will cause a serious fogging and produce disappointing results. Consequently, it is best to attempt the foregoing experiment on a moonless night and well away from any source of artificial light. The heart of a big city is perhaps the poorest location, while rural sites are best. Most first attempts will be followed by a second and often far better record. With some patience anyone may expect a reasonable degree of success.

The stars as individuals will naturally be the objects of interest to many observers and the constellations are the obvious road to finding them.

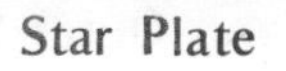

Plate 1: *CIRCUMPOLAR STAR TRAILS.* Photograph courtesy of Lick Observatory.

It would seem clear that some form of naming must be here employed, since one may wish to refer to a particular star to the exclusion of others for some special reason. Methods have been devised in the past in order to accomplish this.

All bright stars and a few faint ones are named by either of two common methods: (1) the first is ages old and refers to an individual star by a proper name, such as Polaris, or Aldebaran, or Castor, etc. Some of these are of Arabic origin, since the Arabs acted as the chief writers and interpreters of astronomical matters during the early Middle Ages. Many such names have definite meanings, such as Polaris (the Pole Star), Sirius (the "searcher" or Dog Star), Deneb (the tail), Aldebaran (the follower), Arcturus (the bear guard). This history of such names becomes one of the very interesting minor portions of astronomy.

(2) The second scheme was introduced in the seventeenth century and employs a Greek letter for each star, coupled with the constellation name, the latter being expressed in the Latin genitive (possessive noun), such as α Alpha Leonis (the constellation of the Lion), β Beta Persei (Perseus, the Hero), γ Gamma Ursae Majoris (the Great Bear), etc. Our charts include these Greek letters, though of course only for certain bright, conspicuous or unusual stars. Alpha, of course, is usually the brightest star in any constellation, Beta the second brightest, and so on.

α	alpha	ι	iota	ρ	rho
β	beta	κ	kappa	σ	sigma
γ	gamma	λ	lambda	τ	tau
δ	delta	μ	mu	υ	upsilon
ϵ	epsilon	ν	nu	ψ	phi
ζ	zeta	ξ	xi	χ	chi
η	eta	ο	omicron	ψ	psi
θ	theta	π	pi	ω	omega

The Greek Alphabet and Signs. Note: Modern usage employs the Greek letter coupled with the accepted constellation abbreviation (see page 52).

A majority of the brightest stars in the heavens have names, so that the beginner need not attempt to use this system until he becomes acquainted with the stars themselves. In some constellations which contain many stars, the Greek letters were exhausted, since there are only twenty-four of them. Some stars were therefore assigned Roman letters, though none of these concern us here. (Greek letters attached to the Big Dipper stars shown on page 51.)

STAR BRIGHTNESS

Any casual observer of the stars has often remarked that they are not all of the same brightness. This was noted early in the history of astronomy and a scale was devised to take care of the apparent differences. We are all familiar with the use of scales to show various comparisons. For example, we indicate age by counting the numbers of years since birth.

On such a scale all numbers are positive. Sometimes it is necessary to think otherwise than in positive terms. Early workers in the field of heat first set up a scale which used the boiling point of water as the highest normal positive point (212° Fahrenheit) and the freezing point of water as a low point (which became 32° on the Fahrenheit scale). When the time came that still lower temperatures were achieved, it was then necessary to extend the scale downward so as to include negative values, such as -20° (or 20° below zero).

Our scale of star brightness is very similar, with the exception of the fact that the positive values denote the fainter degrees of brightness called "magnitudes", while the negative values denote the brighter stars. This resulted from the attempt of the older astronomers to classify all the brightest stars as being of the first magnitude, since they had no means of making careful measures to determine any individual differences among the various stars so classified.

With our modern precise measurements we have found that all the stars formerly classed as the "first magnitude" really belong in still higher values on the scale; so it was necessary to extend the scale upward and include minus values for the brightest objects. As examples we may cite Polaris, whose value is the second magnitude (positive) and Sirius, which is the brightest star in the heavens and has a magnitude of minus 1½ approximately. So accurate have our measurements become that we must also use decimals to show the small differences in brightness between stars that are very nearly alike.

For example, Capella of mag. +0.2 is one-tenth magnitude fainter than Vega, whose value is +0.1. You will find other stars on the charts which are of the third and fourth magnitudes, the comparative brightnesses being roughly shown by the size of the "dot" on the charts. Those fainter than the fourth magnitude are not shown, since their inclusion would tend to confuse the beginner.

No attempt has been made to compare by various sizes of map dots the stars brighter than the first magnitude, but references to the table in the next section will make these apparent. Large differences in brightness will be quickly noticed by the observer, while detection of small ones will require considerable practice.

The normal limit of naked eye visibility is the sixth magnitude, which means that any fainter stars than that value will require optical aid of some kind. Even a pair of good field glasses show a surprising number of additional stars in comparison with those visible to the naked eye, some of these being of even the seventh magnitude. A small telescope may reach the ninth magnitude, while some of the present day giant instruments may reach the twentieth magnitude. Note that the majority of modern faint star work is photographic rather than visual. (See Frontispiece.)

Since the observer will no doubt have his attention drawn to the brighter stars and perhaps may wish for some comparisons between them, a table is presented which includes sixteen bright stars, arranged in order of magnitude, and with their respective distances in light years and their colors as well. They may be easily found with some patience, since all are bright objects. A reasonable goal to be obtained would be a familiarity with ten of the bright stars contained in the table. After learning to recognize them, the student may be surprised to find that they have many colors.

TABLE I: SIXTEEN BRIGHT STARS

Star	Constellation	Mag.	l. y. Dist.	Color
Sirius (Seé-ri-us)	Canis Major	-1.4	8.7	blue-white
Arcturus (Ark-toó-russ)	Bootes	-0.1	36	yellow-orange
Vega (Veé-ga)	Lyra	+0.1	26	blue-white
Rigel (Ryé-gel)	Orion	0.1	650	blue-white
Capella (kah-peĺ-uh)	Auriga	0.2	47	yellow
*Alpha Centauri (Sen-taẃ-ri)	Centaurus	0.3	4.3	yellow
Procyon (Pró-see-un)	Canis Minor	0.4	11	yellow
Altair (Al-taiŕ)	Aquila	0.8	16	white
Aldebaran (Al-deb́-arun)	Taurus	0.8	68	orange
Betelgeuze (Bét-ul-jooz)	Orion	0.9	670	red
Antares (An-taré-eez)	Scorpio	0.9	170	red
Spica (Spý-ka)	Virgo	1.0	150	blue-white
Pollux (Poĺ-uks)	Gemini	1.2	35	yellow
Deneb (Den-eb́)	Cygnus	1.3	540	white
Regulus (Reǵ-you-luss)	Leo	1.3	85	bluish-white
*Fomalhaut (Foaḿ-awl-hawt)	Pisces Australis	1.3	22	white

*Not visible at middle and north latitudes in the United States.

NOTE: Colors indicate temperature, from blue-white (about 20,000° C.) through white, yellow, orange to red (about 3,000° C.)

STAR DISTANCE

It is only after making several observations and obtaining some knowledge of the starry skies that the average observer begins to ask himself questions concerning what he sees. We have already discussed the fact that the stars are not all of equal apparent brightness. Naturally, we may ask about star distances. Astronomers can give very definite data about this question in the light of present day knowledge.

"Are all stars at the same distance away from us?" The answer is a definite "no". Actual calculations of distances show that stars are scattered about in space so that a few are relatively near us, but the great majority are very far away. This is best illustrated by a definition of a satisfactory unit of distance. We cannot employ the mile because the immense distances involved make that unit far too small. The reader may well be reminded that one does not express the distance from New York to San Francisco in inches! By the same token we find that the mile becomes hopelessly inadequate to express any stellar distances.

Astronomers have invented a very useful unit of measurement, which is called the "light year". It is defined as the distance which light, moving with a velocity of 186,000 miles per second, travels in one year of time. This turns out to be about six million million (6,000,000,000,000) miles. Using this light year as our unit of distance, we find that the distance of the nearest star is approximately four light years. To put this in a rather shocking way: as you observe this star this very evening, the light which reaches your eye left the star four years ago! Unfortunately for us, located in the northern latitudes, this star is not visible from the United States and must be seen from a point of observation located farther south. It is named Alpha Centauri.

A good example of the effect of distance may be found in the use of a very well-known and prominent star—Capella. Since its distance is a trifle less than 50 light years, this means the light you would receive this very evening as you observed it, started on its way when Calvin Coolidge had become President. Another startling example of the use of the light year is to be found in the case of β Ursae Majoris, one of the two "pointers" in the Big Dipper. Its distance is approximately 100 light years. Consequently, an observation of the star this very evening would show it as it appeared a hundred years ago; President Grant was in his second term of office.

How are stellar distances determined? The most common method (which was known to the Greeks) is called the "trigonometric", since simple trigonometry is employed. If you will look at Fig. 1, you will see in the diagram

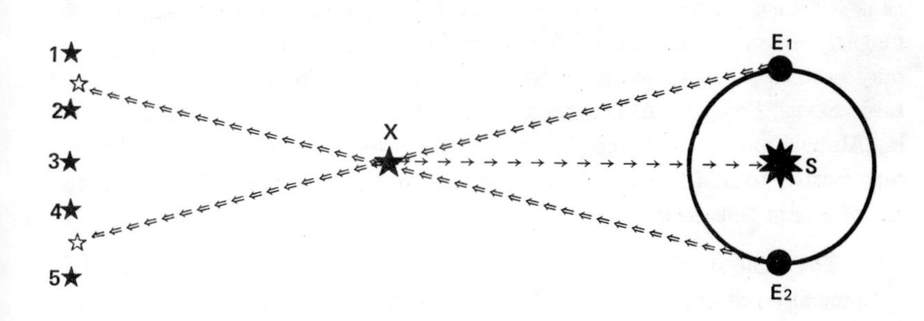

Fig. 1: Measuring Distance of Nearby Star. The diagram is much exaggerated and the parallactic angle always very small. This method is limited to stars within about 300 light years.

a relatively nearby star at X and stars 1, 2, 3, 4 and 5 at an infinitely farther distance. As viewed from the Earth at position E_1 star X seems to be between stars 2 and 3. Six months later it has shifted position and seems to be between stars 3 and 4. The entire shift is E_1 X E_2. If we draw X—S, we then have a right angled triangle in which E_1S is known (as this is the radius of the Earth's orbit) and angle E_1 X S is half the total shift (called the parallactic angle). Simple trigonometry enables us to solve the distance between X (the star) and S (our Sun).

We may add that many stars are distant by immense amounts. It would be safe to say that the light of the majority of the stars you see left the individual stars more than half a century ago! Distances of 500 and even 1000 light years are quite common, while astronomers continually deal with figures on the order of tens of thousands of light years in special cases.

DOUBLE STARS

The average observer may go on the assumption that all stars are individuals and therefore each star should be a single and distinct object. This is indeed true in general, but is not so in many particular cases. Careful observation, usually with high-powered telescopes, shows instances where we have expected to see a single star and where we actually find two stars. Continued observations may show that these two are in some manner physically connected, since they seem to be in motion about each other. Such a pair is properly termed a "double star". In all cases a complete investigation must be made before we have a true double star. This is because two stars may be almost in the same line of sight in space and still have no actual connection, since one may be hundreds of light years beyond the other.

The proper term for a physically related pair of stars is "binary system". Many are now known and in a great number of cases a pair of good field glasses is sufficient to separate the two stars in the system. In other cases greater magnifying power may be needed, such as that obtained with a telescope. It may be of interest to remark that among the sixteen bright stars listed in our table Sirius, Procyon, Aldebaran and Antares are binary systems, while Capella, Alpha Centauri and Regulus constitute triple star systems. However, we may hasten to add that none of them may be shown as multiple without the use of a large telescope.

The table on the opposite page lists a number of interesting double star systems alphabetically by constellations and, for each pair, gives also the approximate magnitudes. Those marked with an * are closer together and more difficult to observe as separate stars than the rest. Some of the more easily located examples are included in our charts. The "," separates magnitudes.

TABLE II: SOME IMPORTANT DOUBLE STARS

* γ	Andromedae	2, 5 mags.	μ	Draconis	5, 5 mags.
* γ	Arietis	5, 5	γ	Leonis	5, 7
* π	Bootis	5, 5	κ	Lepus	4, 6
δ	Cephei	4, 7	ϵ	Lyrae	5, 5
β	Cygni	3, 5	* θ	Serpens	4, 4
* 61	Cygni	6, 6	* ζ	Ursus Majoris	2, 4
* α	Canes Venatici	3, 6	* ζ	Virginis	4, 4
* γ	Delphini	5, 5			

STAR CLUSTERS

We have seen that there are millions of stars, most of which are single objects, but some are double or multiple. While all these are of considerable interest to the student, we must also recognize certain groupings which include some of the most amazing evidences of nature's handiwork, the star clusters. While these require some field glass or telescopic aid for the most part, there are quite a few which are visible without optical help.

A star cluster, as the name indicates, is a group of stars quite closely clustered together in the sky and, as astronomers assure us, clustered in reality as well. We recognize the fact that the members of such a cluster must all be in motion through space at the same rate and in the same direction. Consequently, the only way to ascertain which stars belong to the cluster and which are "field stars" is to check the motion of each star. We can recognize two distinct types, the "open cluster" and the "globular cluster", both described below.

The "open cluster", sometimes called "galactic" because of the tendency toward locations in or very near the Milky Way, ranges in membership from a few dozen to a few hundred stars, all being at the same distance from the Sun and partaking of a common motion. When they are classified according to the number of stars and the degree of concentration toward the center, then all members of a certain cluster have about the same distances as the others in the cluster. We are able to determine the cluster distances by statistical methods. When we do this, as originally done by R.J. Trumpler, we find that the diameters of these objects range from about 5 light years to about 60 light years, while the concentration of stars or their average distance apart is considerably less than the average spacing of stars in the region about the Sun. About 400 of these "open clusters" are known.

Perhaps the most famous open cluster, and, at the same time a naked eye object in the sky, is the Pleiades, found in Taurus (the Bull) (map no. 2, and plate 2). This object is very easily seen with the naked eye and seems to most observers to consist of six or seven stars, though unusually clear skies and sharp eyes may reveal as many as nine. More fortunate observers, located in desert or mountain regions, claim to have detected as many as fifteen stars. At any rate, the number you may see will be a test of a combination of good eyesight and general seeing conditions. Should they be poorly seen on one night, then, by all means, try again, since atmospheric clarity and steadiness are absolute requirements of success.

A good pair of field glasses will show about twenty stars, while even a small telescope will increase this to forty or more. Professional astronomers, by long period photographs, have identified over two hundred stars in this cluster, all being contained within a sphere that is about 40 light years in diameter and about 400 light years distant. The foregoing makes it quite evident just how interesting an object the Pleiades cluster may be and how much its careful study, whether by means of the naked eye, the field glass, or the telescope, may prove a challenge to the observer.

Another splendid example of the open cluster is the famous double cluster in Perseus (map no. 2). Extend the line joining the stars Delta and Alpha (δ and α) about 3 or 4 times and bend it a little eastward toward Andromeda. It is visible to the naked eye on a clear, moonless night; the use of field glasses or a small telescope will bring expressions of amazement, so beautiful is this object.

The second class of clusters is the "globular" type, so called because the arrangement of stars suggests the fact that they would all be concentrated within an imaginary globe (see plate 3). Over one hundred examples are known, having an average diameter on the order of a hundred light years, so that a globular cluster would contain about ten times as many stars per cubic unit of space as the average open cluster. However, the density toward the center is perhaps 100 times as great, since a single globular cluster may contain as many as 100,000 stars!

One of the most remarkable facts about these beautiful objects concerns their distances and distribution. Shapley, by utilizing the period-luminosity curve (see pages 32, 41) for the Cepheids, which are common variable stars in globular clusters, determined their distances from us to range in light years between 18,000 and 180,000. They have the distinction of being the most distant class of objects in the stellar system. Their distribution in the sky is such that the large majority are concentrated in the Sagittarius—Scorpio region (see map 5). The significance of this will be discussed later.

The two naked eye examples of the globular clusters are unfortunately located in the southern skies and consequently invisible to observers within the United States. The brightest in the northern sky is the Hercules cluster, shown in plate 4, and commonly known as Messier 13, after the French observer who first prepared a catalog of prominent clusters and nebulae. As this is definitely a telescopic object, at least field glasses will be necessary for observing it. This cluster is one of the most beautiful and amazing aggregations of stars known to man, being approximately 30,000 light years distant and containing over 50,000 stars! To find it, follow north from β (Beta) Hercules beyond the first bright star you see.

PHYSICAL CHARACTERISTICS

"Are all stars alike?" This question is often put to the astronomer, and his answer is a definite "no". Through the use of an auxiliary instrument called the spectroscope we can show that **99%** of all stars fall into six main classes. These classes show differences in color, temperature and specific physical make-up. At one end of the sequence we have the very hot, bluish stars, which seem to contain considerable amounts of certain gases, of which hydrogen and helium predominate.

At the other end we have relatively cool, reddish stars, whose main constitution seems to be abundant metallic elements, such as iron, calcium and titanium. Some even show evidence of molecular compounds, such as titanium oxide. Midway between these two extremes are such stars as the Sun itself—relatively not very hot, yellowish in color, and containing both gases and some metals in a gaseous state.

The work of collecting this data has occupied over sixty years and now provides data for more than a quarter of a million stars upon which careful studies have been made. Since the majority of the work was done at Harvard, it is commonly called the "Harvard Sequence", and a summary of the main characteristics is shown in the table which follows:

TABLE III: STAR SEQUENCE

Type	*Temp.	Color	**Spectrum	Examples
B	20,000°	bluish	strong H and He	Rigel, Spica
A	10,000°	blue-white	strong H, some metals	Sirius, Vega
F	7,500°	pale yellow	metals stronger	Procyon
G	6,000°	yellow	numerous metallic lines	Sun, Capella
K	4,500°	orange	calcium stronger, metals weaker	Arcturus, Aldebaran
M	3,500°	red	numerous molecular compounds	Betelgeuze, Antares

*NOTE: Temperatures are given in the absolute scale, which has its zero point at -273 degrees C. Otherwise each degree is the same as in the Centigrade scale.

**NOTE: H = Hydrogen; He = Helium

We must not immediately jump to the conclusion that, for example, titanium does not exist in Rigel. Actually, the titanium oxide found in low temperature stars fails to show in the spectrum of Rigel simply because the temperature is too high for it to exist as a compound. Even more baffling is the fact that two stars at about the same surface temperature may have somewhat different spectral lines on the spectrum photograph (spectrogram) that indicate the kinds of elements found in the star, even though the classification of both is the same. It would seem that a logical explanation would be simply that there is a difference in the abundance of elements in some stars as compared with others.

The Harvard Sequence is a very useful guide too, since it enables the astronomer to gain some idea of the variations among stars, at least from a purely physical viewpoint; but there is still another use to which it may be put, which yields the conclusion that stars are not all stamped from an "assembly line" pattern.

SOME COMPARISONS OF STARS

If the brightness of a street lamp is observed as compared with others, we will have a rough analogy to the scale of apparent magnitude, discussed in a previous section; but if we knew how far away from us a certain light is, in comparison with another, then we would be in a position to compare their real brightnesses. It is well-known that a 25 watt lamp gives only a fourth of the light of a 100 watt lamp, if both are at the same distance. In the same manner, if we know the apparent magnitude of a star coupled with its distance, then we are in a position to calculate its real or intrinsic brightness when expressed in terms of a standard of distance (32.6 light years). This is obviously of immense value, since it enables us to make valid comparisons and to then draw conclusions, which in turn have a closeness to truth.

For example, suppose we were to compare Sirius with Alpha Centauri. The former is about four times the apparent brightness of the latter, but this would be modified if we know the respective distances involved. Since we know the distances (8.7 light years to Sirius and 4.3 light years to Alpha Centauri), we can then correct our values of brightness and find that Sirius is actually about 16 times as bright as Alpha Centauri when distance is taken into account.

Such corrected magnitudes are called "absolute" magnitudes, since they are always based upon an absolute standard of distance for comparison purposes.

Even more interesting to us is the "total luminosity" of a star as compared with our own Sun. We are astonished to find that Arcturus has over 100, Capella over 150, Antares over 1000, and Rigel over 30,000 times the luminosity of our Sun. These latter examples would argue the presence of giant stars, since such a large total luminosity must show the existence of a much larger radiating surface. Let us now look into this further.

THE RUSSELL DIAGRAM

Suppose we construct a chart upon which we will enter the absolute magnitude vs. the spectral class of a large number of stars. The horizontal scale will run from class B at the extreme left through A, F, G, K and finally M at the extreme right. The vertical scale will run from the highest absolute magnitude (and luminosity) at the top to very low values at the bottom. The position of each star will be represented as a dot on the chart. When we finish, we will have an arrangement (Fig. 2) called a Russell Diagram (more properly called a Hertzsprung-Russell Diagram), after the astronomers who first constructed it. From this diagram we may draw the following conclusions, although we should have hundreds of stars entered upon it.

(a) A considerable number of stars are placed within a band running from upper left diagonally toward the lower right. None are of extraordinary

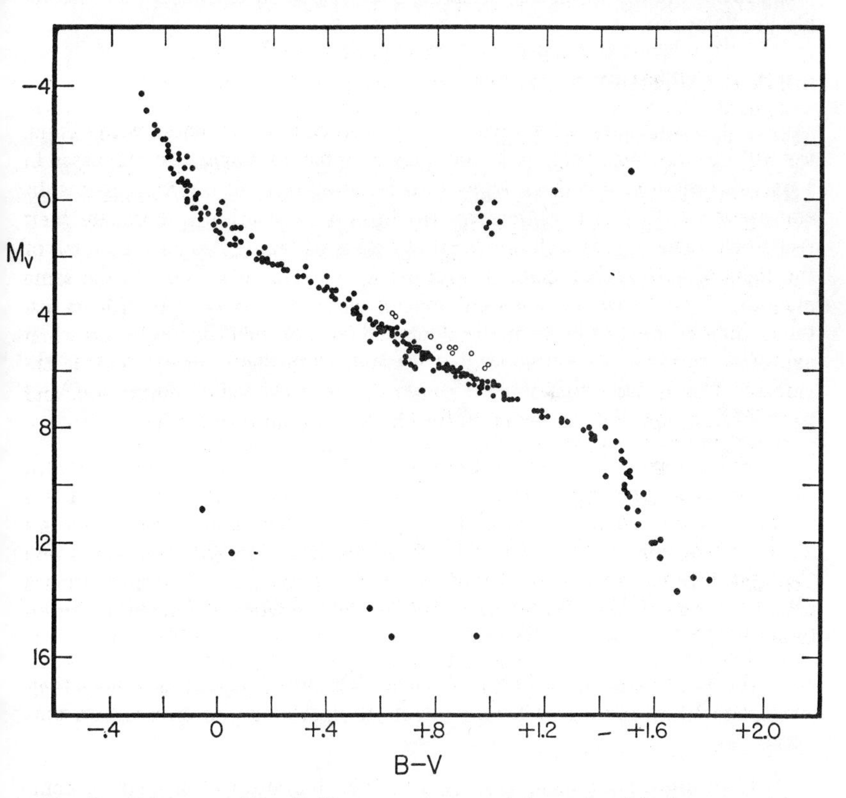

Fig. 2: Hertzsprung-Russell Diagram, constructed for stars with very accurately known distances (Johnson and Morgan). Vertical scale shows absolute magnitude. Horizontal scale shows the color index, from blue at left to red at right. Note the main sequence diagonally spread across the chart (where the bulk of the stars are found). The few white dwarfs appear on the lower left, while the few orange and red giants appear on the upper right. No super-giants are shown. (Copyright 1953, Univ. of Chicago Press.)

brilliance. They are called the "main sequence" stars and really are of moderate or of low luminosities, the Sun being one of them. We commonly call them "dwarfs" because their moderate luminosities do not require a very large radiating surface.

(b) A number of stars of quite considerable luminosities run from left to right horizontally and are called "giants" because their higher values of radiation will require a greater surface.

(c) Across the top is still another, though smaller, group of extremely high luminosity stars. These are termed "super-giants", for they are truly exceptional in terms of total luminosity and size.

(d) At the left and below is an isolated group of a few "mavericks" called "white dwarfs", because they are hot stars but at the same time small. The companion of Sirius, called Sirius B, is an example.

While giant and super-giant stars are of considerable interest, their numbers, as compared with the main sequence group, are quite small. The most significant thing to us is that such stars must be truly gigantic in proportions, since the total radiation from a star depends upon two things: temperature and size (surface). If we compare a super-giant like Betelgeuze (reddish, low temperature, absolute magnitude -5½) with the Sun (yellow, moderate temperature, absolute magnitude slightly less than +5), we can immediately see that the large energy output from the former must be due to unusual size, since its temperature is actually lower.

Betelgeuze could easily swallow our Sun, along with Mercury, Venus, the Earth, and Mars, all being, in their respective orbits, inside its diameter. Its overall size is about 500 times that of the Sun. Such conclusions have been checked by the use of an especially designed instrument called the interferometer, which allows us actually to measure the sizes of giant stars.

COLOR-MAGNITUDE

Color-magnitude comparisons are often made in analyzing the stars that are members of a cluster. This is necessary because we often cannot determine the individual absolute magnitudes, since such a cluster is at a considerable distance. However, we may, without serious error, consider all the stars of a cluster to be at the same distance from the Sun and therefore consider the apparent magnitudes to give a fair idea of the respective luminosities. Since the stars are also too faint to obtain direct spectral classifications, we may simply determine the color.

The resulting diagram is termed a color-magnitude diagram and is thus a substitute for the Russell Diagram in cluster research (Fig. 3). Here we are interested in the kind of stars which exist in a given cluster, since we would like to know if a given cluster is completely homogeneous or is not. For example, the Pleiades show a sequence running from fairly bright-blue stars to fairly

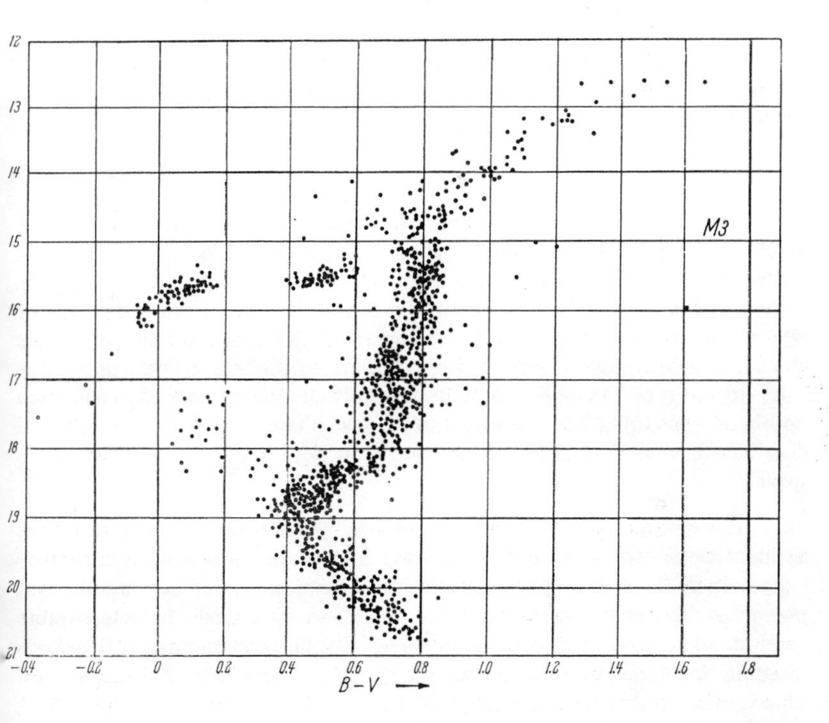

Fig. 3: Color-Magnitude Diagram drawn for the globular cluster M .3 in Canes Venatici, the Hunting Dogs. This small constellation consists of only two clearly visible stars and is found directly under the tip of the handle of the Big Dipper. Courtesy of *"Sky and Telescope".*

faint reddish stars and including a few red giants. Others differ in containing some stars which are excessively hot. Observations and diagrams enable us to speculate as to the age of such clusters and to report that some are relatively young, while still others are relatively old because the excessively hot stars are no longer present, having become modified into cooler stars through advancing age.

The globular clusters seem to be populated only by giants and super-giants. This is because such objects are at such distances that normal main sequence stars are too feeble to show up. At any rate, we are inclined to believe that the globular clusters are of advanced age, since both giant size and orange or reddish color are signs of the dying out of a star.

We wonder and are amazed at the existence of the giant and super-giant stars. At the same time we must not overlook the fact that the majority of stars are main sequence (dwarf) stars, and that the Sun would be no better than "average" on its "report card"!

An interesting figure here is number 10,000. This is because of its usefulness in illustrating extremes. The great super-giants would outshine our Sun by a ratio of about 10,000 to 1. On the other hand, some stars are so feeble in their total output of energy that this would be only 1/10,000 of the Sun's energy!

MOTION

"Are the stars fixed in space?" Definitely "no". As far as we can tell, all stars, the Sun included, are traveling through space. Some are doing so at a very leisurely pace, while others are really in quite a hurry. Do not be concerned about the chances of a collision. So great is the average distance of separation that the chances of a collision are to all intents and purposes none at all. The best way of getting this great spread of distance well in mind is this: if you took the huge Grand Central Station in New York City and emptied it of everything but a few specks of dust, then those few specks, if well distributed, would be relatively much nearer together than the stars are in space!

The determination of motion is made by the use of the spectroscope, an instrument for analyzing the light rays from a star. If the star is approaching us, then the entire spectrum (the total arrangement of the various light rays of a star) is shifted toward the violet end by a small, but measurable amount, which is proportional to the speed. In the same manner, if the star is receding, then the entire spectrum is shifted to the red end of the spectrum. This is called the "Doppler Effect", after the physicist who first announced it as a principle in physics.

In order to understand this, consider yourself at a railroad station. The train arrives and after it passes you will note that the pitch of the bell sound becomes lower. This is because less and less vibrations are received by the ear per second, since the distance between the source and the observer is increasing.

A similar effect takes place in light. If a source (star) is receding, then less and less light vibrations are received per second because of increasing distance. Therefore, the frequency of the light diminishes and, since frequency and wave length are inversely related, then the latter increases and becomes slightly greater; or, what is the same thing, each normal wave length is lengthened and the entire spectrum is shifted. The amount of the shift is proportional to the velocity of motion of the source. Note that if a source is moving at right angles to the line of sight there can be no Doppler Effect, since the distance is neither increasing or decreasing.

The Sun also is in motion, traveling through space at the leisurely pace of 12 miles per second with respect to the framework of stars about it. Any space velocities of stars, as determined from the Doppler Effect, always are corrected for the Sun's motion so that they are referred to the Sun as if it were at rest.

Why are the stars in motion? As we will see later, all stars form a gigantic system and these space motions are due to the behavior of the individual stars within the system itself.

VARIABLE STARS

Although the great majority of stars do not change in their brightness, there are nevertheless a considerable number which do, and the study of these is without doubt one of the most fruitful and one of the most interesting portions of astronomy as a whole. As early as the seventeenth century certain careful observers had noticed that some stars fluctuated in their brightnesses. As early as perhaps the beginning Chinese dynasties the scholars left records of sudden "blazing stars". Several of the astronomers of the Middle Ages recorded a series of observations upon a "star which appeared where before there was none to be seen". In recent years the total number of such unusual stars which have been recognized and catalogued has increased greatly. Now the study of such objects is considered to be a special branch of the science of astronomy.

A "variable star" is one which shows definite variations in the intensity of its light, as measured by some acceptable standards. Some stars require but a few hours or perhaps a few days to complete their variations; others may require months or even years. Still others seemingly do not have a definite period of regularity and are consequently classed as "irregular".

The amount of change in some cases is very slight. In others it may be so much as to cause the star to be visible to the naked eye at some times and to be out of reach of all but the largest telescopes at other times.

The credit for the discovery of many of these interesting objects must be divided. Amateur observers have been successful in their patient searches in many cases. Professional astronomers have been responsible for many discoveries, usually because of the large amount of good equipment at their command. In some cases the variability has been demonstrated by amateurs, whereas the actual detailed computation and further investigation has been in the hands of professional astronomers. Photography has greatly enlarged the field, and has given sequences of plates in some cases.

A variable star, or simply "a variable", is usually given some special designation after its variability has been demonstrated, provided that it does not already bear the usual Greek letter designation of a well-known star. For example, we have such variables as δ Delta Cephei, η Eta Aquilae and o Omicron Ceti, and these require no further special note. However, the less well-known stars are usually given a special Roman letter, or even a double letter, both prefixed to the constellation name. Examples are: R Leonis, RR Lyrae, SS Cygni. In some cases all single and double letters in combination have been exhausted so that serial numbers combined with the letter "v" are used, such as v366 Cygni.

The character of the variation is obtained by plotting numerous observations which are well scattered as to dates and times. After this plotting is done as accurately as possible, then a smooth curve is fitted mathematically to the observations. The result is termed the "light curve", two examples of which are shown in Fig. 4 below.

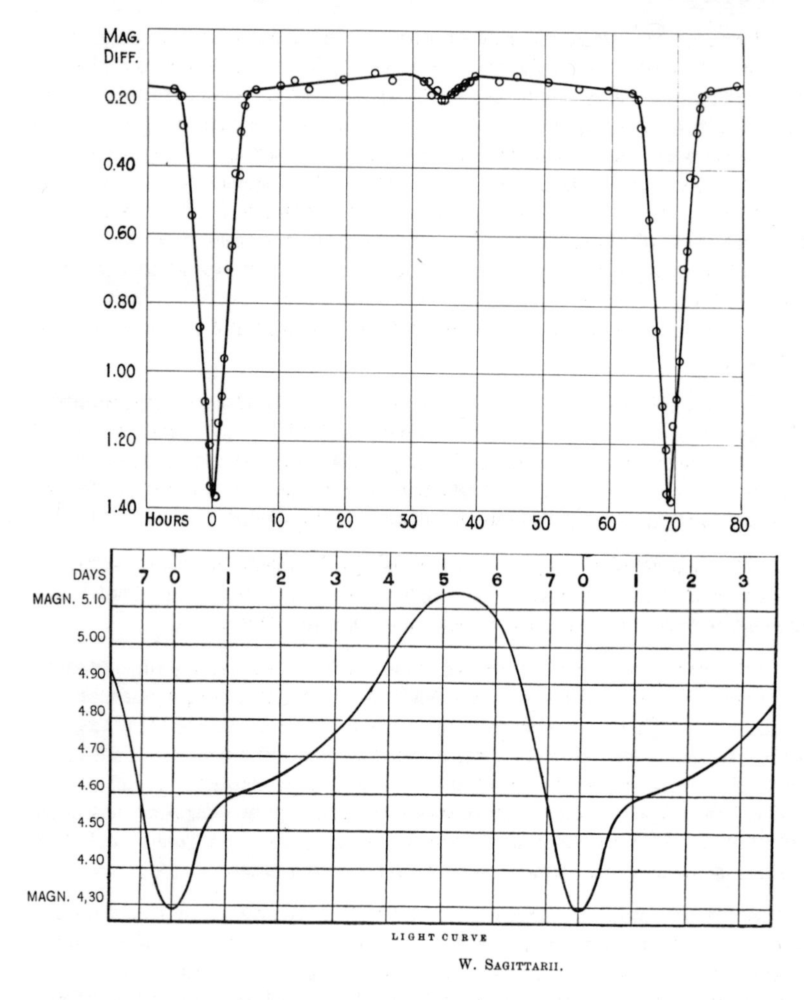

Fig. 4: Light Curves of Two Variable Stars, Algol in the constellation Perseus (map 2), and W Sagittarii, in the constellation Sagittarius. The curve of Algol covers 68 hours, while the curve of W Sagittarii is for 7 days.

The complete cycle of fluctuation (from maximum light back to maximum light or from minimum light to minimum light) is called the "period" and may be anything from a few hours to several years. In the examples illustrated the periods are approximately 68 hours and 7½ days respectively. Obviously, an "irregular" variable will have no real period and this may be shown by plotting a great many observations, which are scattered without any logical pattern.

After studying many variable stars, the astronomers have been able to group them into a number of well-established classes. Here we must carefully distinguish between the periodic type, which has a definite and well-established period of fluctuation, and the irregular type, which has no definite period. In the paragraphs to follow we discuss briefly three groups: (a) the Cepheids; (b) the long period class; (c) the Novae. Of these the first two are periodic (the light fluctuating at periodic intervals), while the third class is non-periodic.

(a) The Cepheid class was named from Cephei (Cepheus is a constellation between Cygnus, the Swan, and the North Pole), which was the first variable star discovered in the group. These stars usually have periods which are relatively short (from a few hours to about two months). Some of them are visible to the naked eye and include δ Cephei, η Aquilae and ζ Geminorum. In most cases the variation is only about one full magnitude. Observations made by the layman must of necessity require patience, as he will not usually know exactly when to expect the changes which occur.

(b) A second class of variables has perhaps the most interest to the beginner. This is the long period class, whose members require a variation of several months to two years to complete the cycle of variation, the majority being about 300 days. The range of variation is usually quite large, being as much as eight magnitudes in some cases. Another special characteristic of stars in the long period class is their decidedly red color.

The best known star of the long period group is Omicron Ceti, commonly known as "Mira" or "the wonderful", as it was named by the Arabs. It is found in the constellation of Cetus, the Whale (see map 7). This star variously reaches the second or third magnitude at maximum brightness when it is easily visible to the naked eye. At minimum it appears far below naked eye visibility, usually reaching the ninth magnitude. The variation in light of this star stretches over a period of 331 days.

There are many long period variables now known and under continuous observation. An additional feature of all of them, which is indeed odd, is the variation of physical characteristics along with the variation of brightness. Still another puzzling characteristic is that of failing to reproduce the light curve and variations exactly, but at the same time reproducing it approximately.

(c) The third group of variable stars is perhaps the most amazing of all. Imagine a star which has been relatively inconspicuous and with no suspicion of variable behavior. Suddenly, without any warning, it blazes up to a brilliant maximum brightness, usually in a matter of hours rather than days. It remains at this peak for a very short time and then begins a slow descent in brightness with numerous irregularities in the plotted curve.

Such a star is called a "Nova", since it was originally believed that the star was actually new. Most novae have been positively identified with stars already known, so that such a view is no longer taken seriously. However, there is one way in which we may consider the star new. This is in the sense that some remarkable change has taken place in the star itself, especially since observations show an increase in brightness on the order of 50,000 times and, in extreme cases, of 100,000 times!

This enormous increase in the brightness is no doubt the result of some release of a large amount of energy in a very short time. The complete explanation is still one of the baffling problems of modern astronomy, although we are now fairly certain that a subatomic process is responsible and that such processes are likewise responsible for the energy of all stars.

A nova is always designated by the word "Nova" followed by the constellation name and the year of outburst. A few examples are: Nova Persi 1901, which rose to magnitude 0.1; Nova Aquilae 1918, which reached minus 1.1 and which was, at that time, the second brightest star in the sky. A nova in the year 1572 was observed to equal the brightness of the planet Venus (or approximately -4.0) and was visible in daylight!

Many an interested layman wishes to make observations of scientific value. There is no better or more fascinating field for this than the observation of variable stars, especailly of the long-period class. There are many examples well within the reach of even the simplest equipment, such as field glasses. The work is relatively easy and directions are obtainable from observers already in the field. In the United States these are banded together as the *American Association of Variable Star Observers*, with their headquarters at Cambridge, Massachusetts. Additions to their membership are cordially welcomed and a full explanation of the method employed, with appropriate maps, are available. Reports of the observations, along with current pertinent news in the field are printed regularly.

Anyone with a reasonable amount of patience will find that the observations are not too time consuming and are very simple to make. The method employed may be termed the method of comparison. For example, let us suppose we are making an estimate of the brightness of a fictitious variable star we will call "v". Let us suppose that we refer to a map of the field of surrounding stars, and that there are three whose brightnesses are closest to that of the variable. Suppose star "a" has a brightness of 6.0 mag., star "b" of 6.4 mag. and star "c" of 7.0 mag. Looking carefully at "v" we see that it is certainly fainter than "a" and that the brightness lies somewhere between "b" and "c".

The problem then resolves itself into just where we will make the estimate between 6.4 and 7.0. If we decide the variable lies about midway between these two, we will set it down as 6.7. Should we decide its brightness is somewhat nearer the brighter of the two comparison stars, then we will set it down as 6.5 or 6.6. With practice it is surprising how accurate one may become in the application of this method. At the same time there is considerable satisfaction in doing work of real scientific value.

A complete table of variable stars would be very imposing, as so many of these interesting objects are known. Since the beginner is just becoming acquainted with them, so to speak, a brief list is included so as to enable him to make a start by observing some of them often enough to satisfy himself of their variability. Some do not remain at naked eye brightness during their entire period, of course, and therefore may only be observed during part of the cycle. Still others may remain at a certain level of brightness for months or even years at a time and then suddenly fluctuate noticeably without warning. The unannounced changes will furnish the average observer with many a thrill in the detection of the sudden variation at a time of mere routine checking.

Shown below is a list of important variable stars alphabetically by constellations, their range of variation in magnitudes, and the approximate period in days between one maximum and the following maximum.

TABLE IV: SOME IMPORTANT VARIABLE STARS

Star	Range	Period	Star	Range	Period
Gamma Aquilae	3.7-4.4	7 days	Delta Librae	4.8-6.2	2 days
Delta Cephei	3.6-4.3	5 days	Beta Lyrae	3.4-4.3	13 days
Omicron Ceti (Mira)	3-10	332 days	Beta Persei	2.3-3.5	3 days
R Corona Borealis	6-12	irreg.	Beta Pegasi	2.2-27	irreg.
Chi Cygni	4.14	413 days	Rho Persei	3.3-4.2	irreg.
Zeta Geminorum	3.7-4.4	10 days	Lambda Tauri	3.8-4.1	4 days
Eta Geminorum	3.2-4.2	235 days	S Sagittae	5.4-6.1	8 days
Alpha Herculis	3.1-3.9	irreg.			

Some of the above may be found on our charts.

In connection with the light changes in variable stars is the problem of explaining just exactly what causes such changes. In some cases this is a comparatively easy matter. In others it is very difficult or even impossible with our present knowledge.

One of the simpler examples is that of Algol or β Beta Persei (Fig. 4 and map 2). Here we notice that the star seems to be at maximum brightness most of the time, but, at regular intervals, the light decreases very rapidly and rather quickly recovers its former value. In addition there is a slight but quite marked decrease in between any two major decreases. The theory which has been proposed to explain this variation (and others of similar kind) supposed that the star is not really one star but two, and that these are quite dissimilar in diameter and total light.

Suppose that A gives out the most light, but is the smaller of the two, and that B is relatively less bright, but larger. It should be clear that B may seriously eclipse A by moving in front of it and cutting off most of the light, while, at the same time, giving off very little of the total light itself. In the same manner, when A moves in front of B, the light is cut down very little, since the former is responsible for the larger amount of the total light of the system. Astronomers have charted and identified over a thousand systems of this kind and they are commonly known as "eclipsing" stars. Algol is the oldest known, having first been carefully studied in 1783. We must remark in passing that Algol and other similar cases are no longer regarded as true variable stars, since the variability is not due to any real change in the output of energy in the stars. They are really binary systems whose presence is shown by eclipses.

Other types of variation are not so easily explained, as for example the Cepheid Variables. Here the present tentative explanation is based upon a normal balance between the inward pull of gravity and the outward pressure of the hot gases which make up the star's atmosphere. If this balance is upset, the star would become cooler upon expansion and also slightly redder in color. If the balance is upset in the opposite direction, the star would become hotter and therefore brighter and bluer in color. The long period or red variables may also be included in this "pulsating theory". On the other hand, the explanation of the irregular type of variables cannot be considered as complete or satisfactory at present.

While variable stars are always objects of wonder and while adequate explanations of their behavior present a distinct challenge to the astronomer, there is still another matter of more than ordinary interest in connection with one of the classes of variables. What is more, it presents a relationship which is of tremendous value to the astronomer in attempting to obtain the distances of stars or stellar objects which lie beyond the reach of ordinary methods of measuring stellar distances.

Over a half century of Cepheid studies have shown that there is a relationship between the brightness and the period of variation of these variable stars. That is, the fainter Cepheids have shorter periods, while those variable stars which are brighter have longer periods. In other words, the longer the period, the greater is the intrinsic brightness of the star. Indeed, this relationship seems to be so definite that we can actually plot out enough examples to show the existence of the "period-luminosity curve". Obviously, this would be a valuable measuring stick for objects too far away to permit measuring distance by ordinary methods; for all we need is to observe the period in a given case and, with the use of the period-luminosity curve we can then read off the absolute magnitude, which can then be converted into distance.

Plate 2: *THE PLEIADES,* the Pleiades are also called "the Seven Sisters", because of the seven brightest stars, which legend says have fled into the sky to escape from Orion, the Giant Hunter, and are being guarded from him by Taurus, the Bull. Photograph courtesy of Lick Observatory.

Plate 3: *GLOBULAR STAR CLUSTER,* M. 3, in CANES VENATICI (the Hunting Dogs). Photograph courtesy of Lick Observatory.

Plate 4: *GLOBULAR STAR CLUSTER,* M. 13, in HERCULES. (See Star Map number 5). Visible with field glasses or telescope. Photograph courtesy of Lick Observatory.

Plate 5: *STAR CLOUDS* in the MILKY WAY. Photograph courtesy of the Lick Observatory.

Plate 6: *THE ORION NEBULA* (gaseous). Photograph courtesy of Lick Observatory.

Plate 7: *THE LAGOON NEBULA* in SAGITTARIUS (a gaseous nebula). Photograph courtesy of Lick Observatory.

Plate 8: *NORTH AMERICAN NEBULA* in CYGNUS (a gaseous nebula). Photograph courtesy of Lick Observatory.

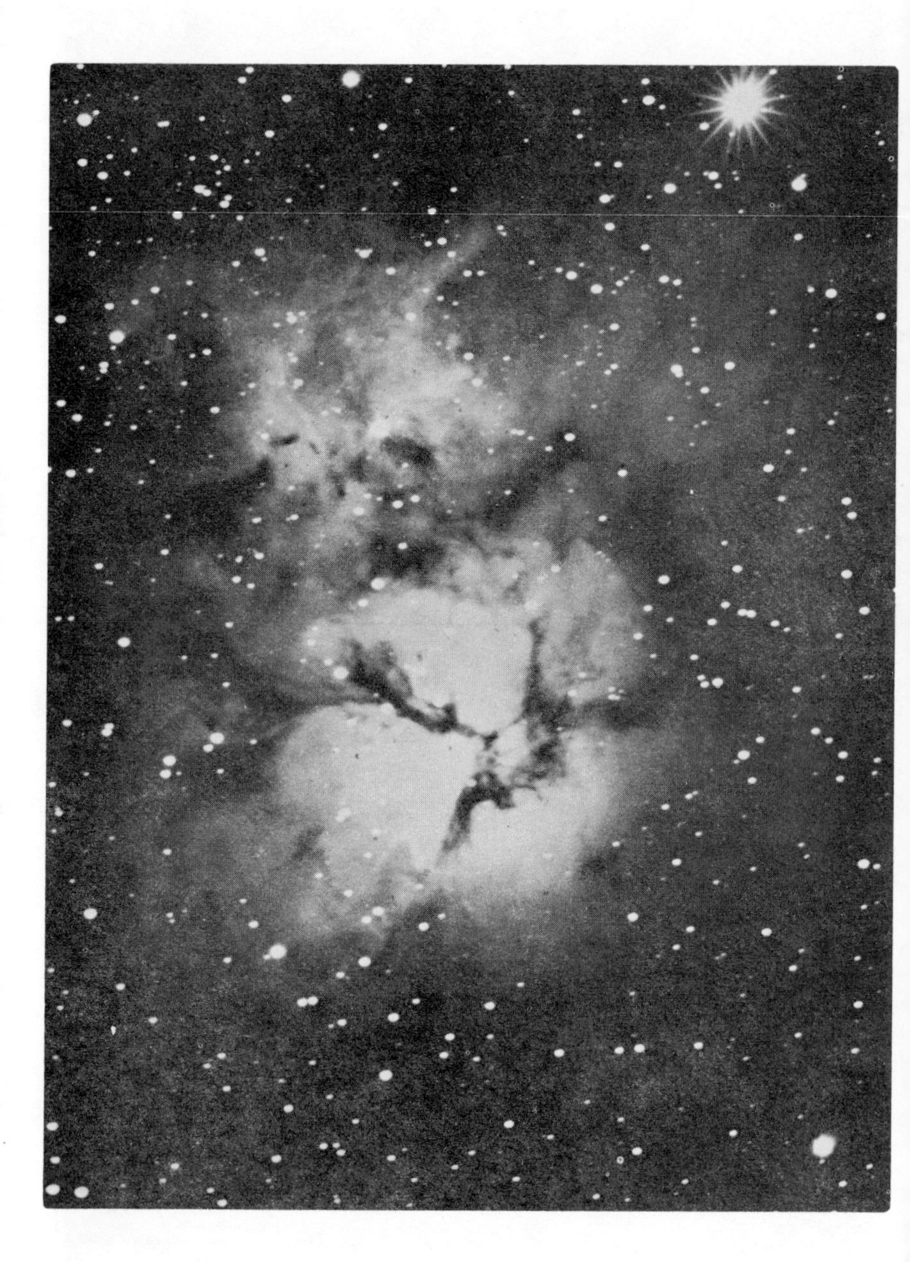

Plate 9: *TRIFID NEBULA,* M. 8, in SAGITTARIUS. Dark material has split this white gaseous nebula into three parts. Photograph courtesy of Lick Observatory.

In practice astronomers have really found two subgroups of Cepheid variables. Type I Cepheids have periods between 1½ and 40 days, brighten quite rapidly and are generally brighter stars (nearly two absolute magnitudes brighter) than the Type II Cepheids. A good example is δ Delta Cephei, easily observed with the naked eye.

Type II Cepheids have periods between 10 and 28 days, the most of them being in the neighborhood of 17 days. Their light curve is very different, having a distinct "kink" or plateau in the declining portion. Type example is W Virginis, which never reaches naked eye visibility.

The determination of distances is one of the most important problems in astronomy. Ordinary methods (see page 17) have their limitations. Consequently, the use of the period-luminosity relationship is of great value and we shall see in a later section how valuable an aid it is in the solution of distance problems.

NOVAE

In addition to the Cepheid type variable stars noted above, there exist still another group showing an astonishing behavior as stated previously on pages 29 and 30. These are stars which increase in brightness very rapidly without warning, remain bright for but a very short time and then commence a very slow but irregular descent for a matter of months or even years. We may call them "eruptive" or "explosive" stars and we designate any of them by the term Nova usually followed by the name of the constellation of which one is located and the year of the outburst. Example: Nova Aquilae 1918, which for a short time equaled the brightness of Sirius, the brightest star in the sky. In most cases we may fortunately have taken a photograph of the star long before the outburst and find that the star was relatively ordinary and often relatively faint. The increase in brightness may be as much as 50,000 times. The lengthy return to the original state is quite irregular. The entire process, when accompanied by studies of the spectral behavior, suggests that some kind of instability results in the release of internal energy in a very short time and a "blow off" at the surface of gases in the form of an envelope or shell which generally disappears after a few years. In a very few cases the process may take place more than once to a certain star. Lest we hastily conclude that novae are to be found only among the stars of our own galaxy, we shall find evidence to the contrary, as shown in the next section.

SUPERNOVAE

During the year AD 1054 the calendar computer of a Chinese emperor reported the appearance of what he quaintly called a "guest star" in the constellation of Taurus. This must represent a nova of unusual violence, since we now find in its place an interesting and irregular shell of expanding gas called the Crab Nebula. Spectrum analysis indicates that the outer filaments contain hydrogen, helium and other elements expanding at about 700 miles per second! Such a rare manifestation is termed a "supernova", since the behavior and certain other characteristics are far greater than in an ordinary nova. Two others are known to have been seen by astronomers before the invention of the telescope, viz.: Tycho's in Cassiopeia (1572) and Kepler's in Ophiuchus (1604). In both cases we have been able to locate and photograph the remnants. Other such supernovae are found in distant stellar systems.

PULSARS

Before attempting to understand these remarkable objects, we must digress for a moment and discuss briefly the subject of atomic structure. Physicists tell us that all substances (solid, liquid or gaseous) are composed of atoms, which are the building blocks of all material. What is an atom? It is composed basically of three different constituents, viz: protons, electrons and neutrons (there are really a few others, but they are neglected in this simplified explanation). The electron is exceedingly small and has a very small mass itself, but is important because it carries a negative electric charge. The proton has 1,836 times the mass of the electron and carries a positive charge. The neutron is odd in the fact that it has about the same mass of the proton, but no charge at all.

Let us take the simplest atom known, that of hydrogen gas. It is composed of one proton plus one electron, but the latter may occupy various positions. We may visualize this in the pattern proposed by the Danish physicist Niels Bohr in 1913. He considered the proton to occupy the central position and the electron any one of other positions. In this simple outline we will not discuss the behavior of the electron as it jumps from one "orbit" to another or falls back from one to another. What is important to us is this: all elements have been classified in three ways; these are (a) the atomic number (number of protons and an equal number of electrons). For hydrogen it is 1, while for helium it is 2; (b) the atomic weight, which is the mass of the atom on a scale with a reference base of oxygen at 16 (hydrogen 1.006, helium 4.003); (c) mass number is the sum of its protons and its neutrons. Since hydrogen has no neutrons, its number is 1, but helium with an atomic number 2 and weight of 4 gets this number because it has two neutrons to add such weight to the two protons.

An atom in its normal state is termed "neutral", since its electrons exactly balance the total positive charge of its protons. An atom which has lost an electron through collision or other means is called "ionized". The escaped electron is called "free".

It does not take much imagination to realize that some of the very complicated atoms may exist in a variety of states; if we carry this line of thought to its extreme, is it possible that a star, which normally is composed of protons, electrons and neutrons, might exist entirely without the first two—in other words, become entirely composed of neutrons?

In 1965 a group of observers at the University of Cambridge astonished the astronomical world by the discovery of an entirely new class of objects. The peculiar thing was their regular emission of bursts of radio noise. So accurately were such outbursts timed and so short were their periods that one of them had a period of ¼ second and the graphical representation used a scale measured in milliseconds (thousandths of a second)! They were called "pulsars" because the rapid "beats" were similar to heartbeats. One of the important results of observation was that all were quite faint. This suggested that they were quite small or relatively cold or both.

The first natural explanation was that these stars were white dwarfs, but on various grounds this was finally rejected. There remained but one other reasonable explanation. They were neutron stars! Obviously, such a star has evolved from an "original" star of perhaps average makeup. The process may be difficult to work out, but its consideration is a part of the entire problem of the birth, life and death of a star.

CONCLUSION

So far we have devoted our entire attention to the stars as individuals. We have shown how to find them, something of their physical makeup, their distance, sizes, brightnesses, temperatures, colors, and behaviors. We have also emphasized that all stars are not constructed out of the same mold, or assembly line process. Let us now turn our attention to a consideration of the stars as a total assembly or system. Also we will discuss the possible life cycle of a star.

Plate 10: *"OWL" NEBULA* in URSA MAJOR, M. 97. Photograph courtesy of Lick Observatory.

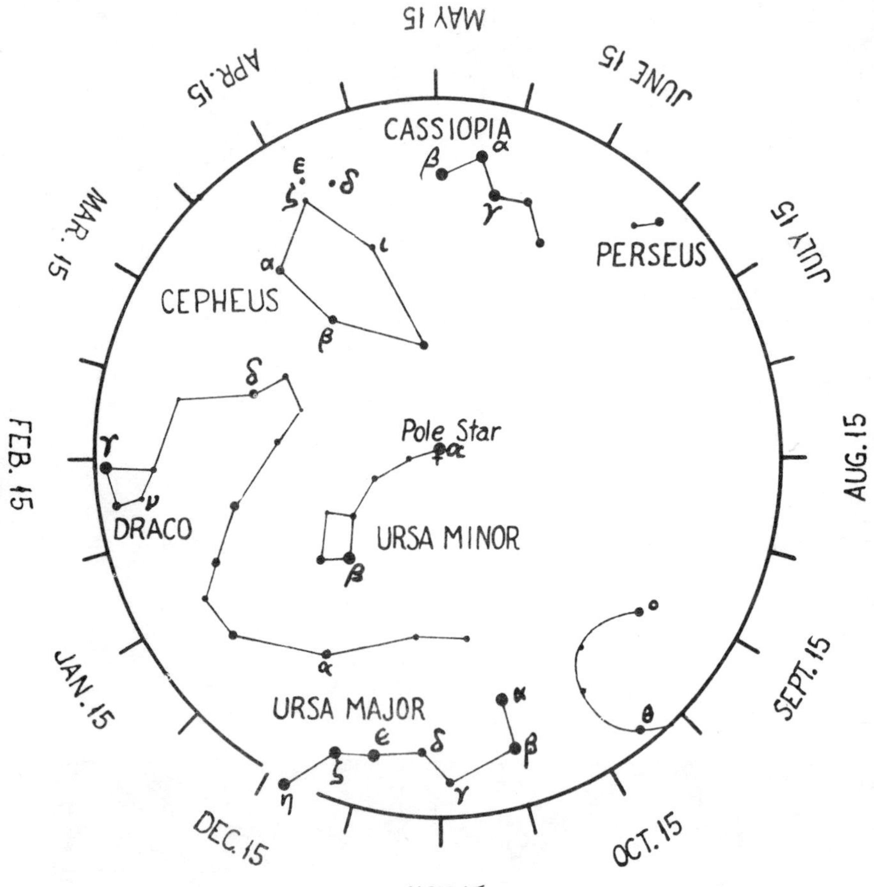

1 *CIRCUMPOLAR CONSTELLATIONS*

DIRECTIONS FOR THE USE OF THE STAR MAPS

1. Determine the direction of NORTH in your observing location.
2. Orient Map 1 so that the date corresponding to time of year is DOWNWARD.
3. The circumpolar constellations will then appear as shown on the map.
4. Turn about and face SOUTH, having selected another map of appropriate date and time.
5. Those constellations in the southeast, south and southwest will appear as shown.

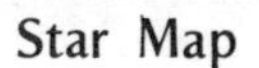

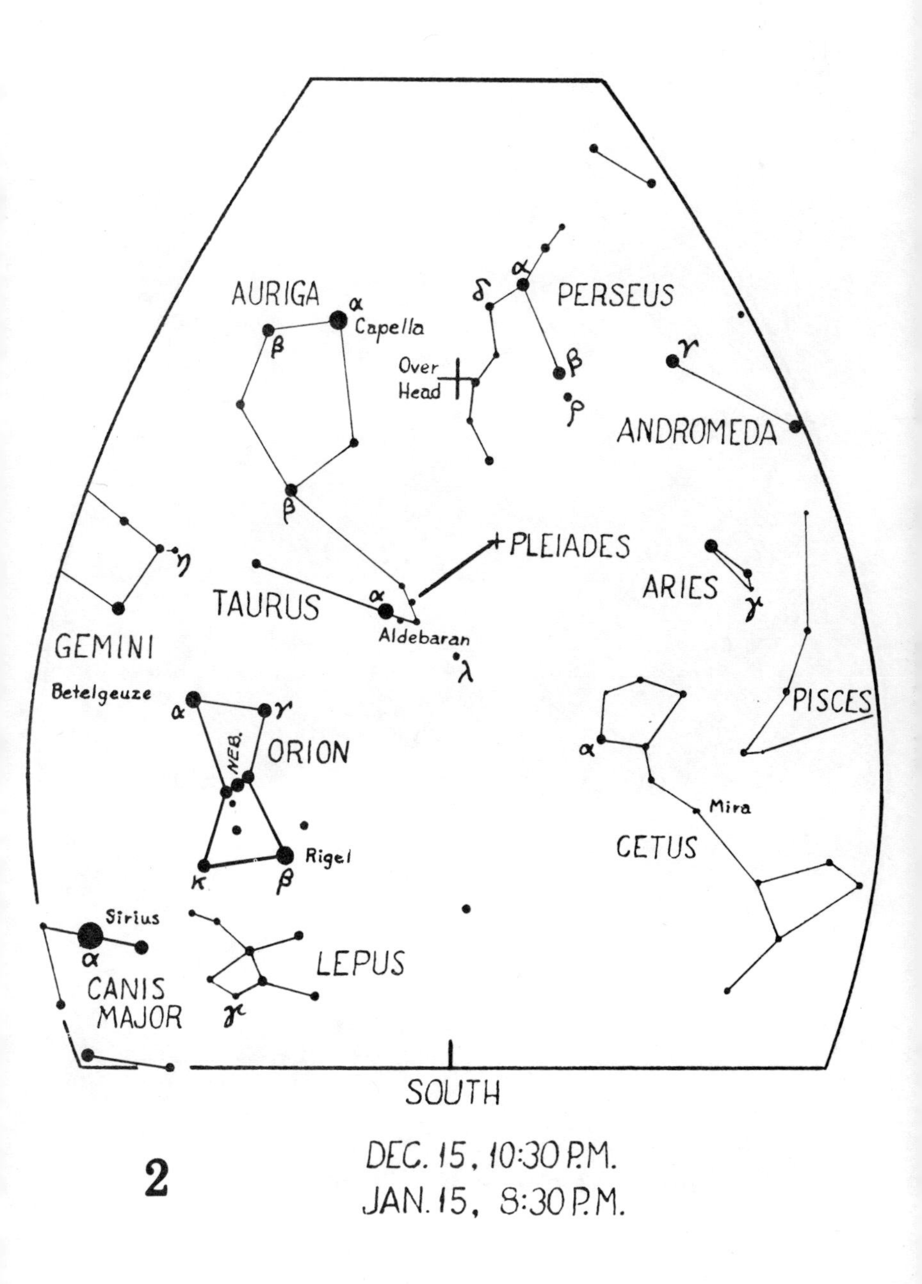
AURIGA
α
Capella
β
β
Over
Head
δ
α
PERSEUS
β
ρ
γ
ANDROMEDA
η
PLEIADES
ARIES
γ
TAURUS
α
Aldebaran
λ
GEMINI
Betelgeuze
α
γ
NEB.
ORION
Rigel
κ
β
α
PISCES
Mira
CETUS
Sirius
α
CANIS
MAJOR
LEPUS
γ
SOUTH
2
DEC. 15, 10:30 P.M.
JAN. 15, 8:30 P.M.

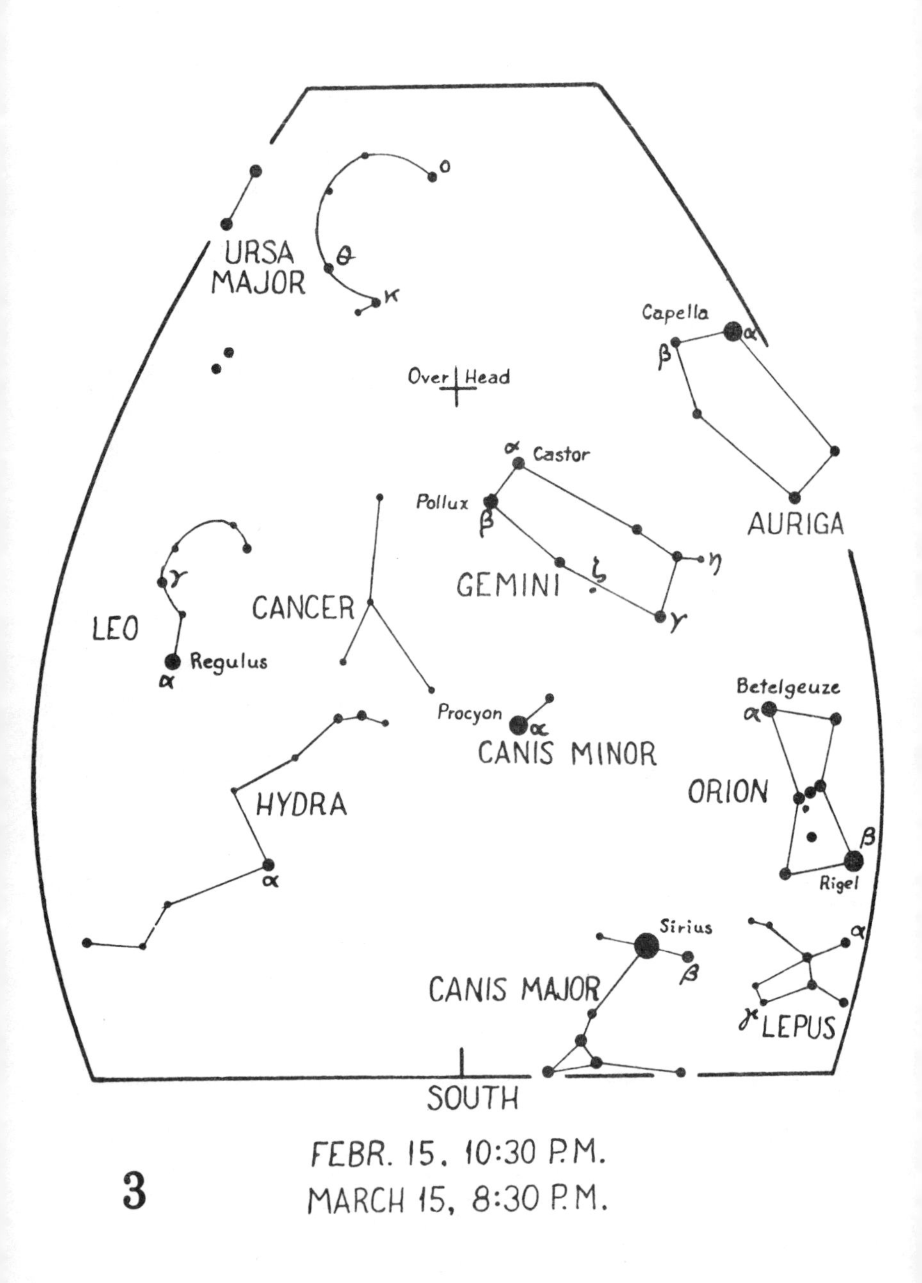
URSA
MAJOR
Over Head
Capella
Castor
Pollux
AURIGA
GEMINI
LEO
CANCER
Regulus
Procyon
CANIS MINOR
Betelgeuze
ORION
HYDRA
Rigel
Sirius
CANIS MAJOR
LEPUS
SOUTH
FEBR. 15. 10:30 P.M.
MARCH 15, 8:30 P.M.
3

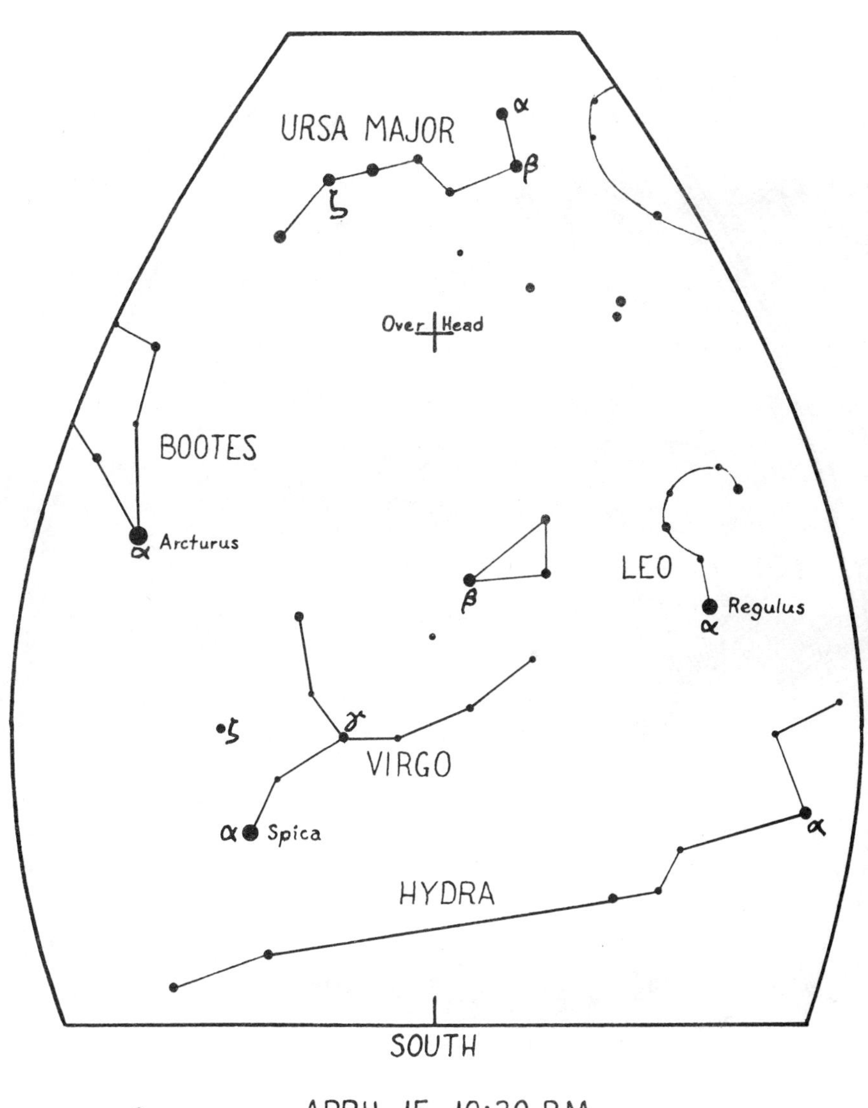

4

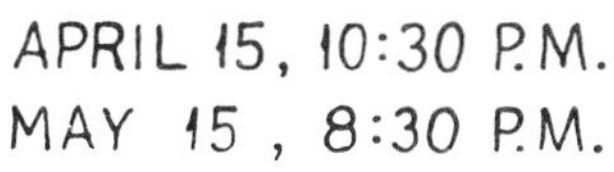
APRIL 15, 10:30 P.M.
MAY 15, 8:30 P.M.

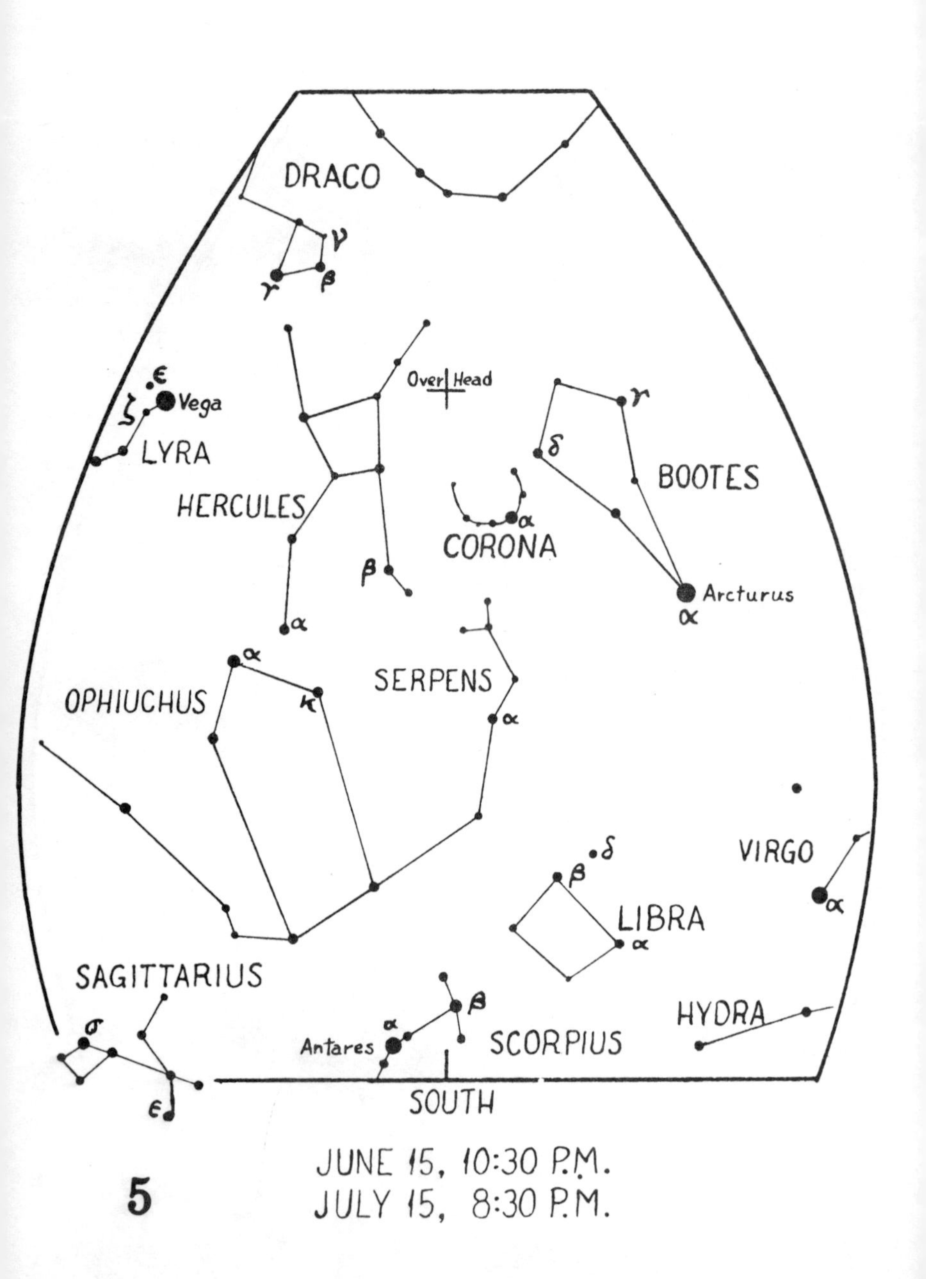
DRACO
Over Head
LYRA
Vega
HERCULES
CORONA
BOOTES
Arcturus
OPHIUCHUS
SERPENS
VIRGO
LIBRA
SAGITTARIUS
Antares
SCORPIUS
HYDRA
SOUTH
JUNE 15, 10:30 P.M.
JULY 15, 8:30 P.M.
5

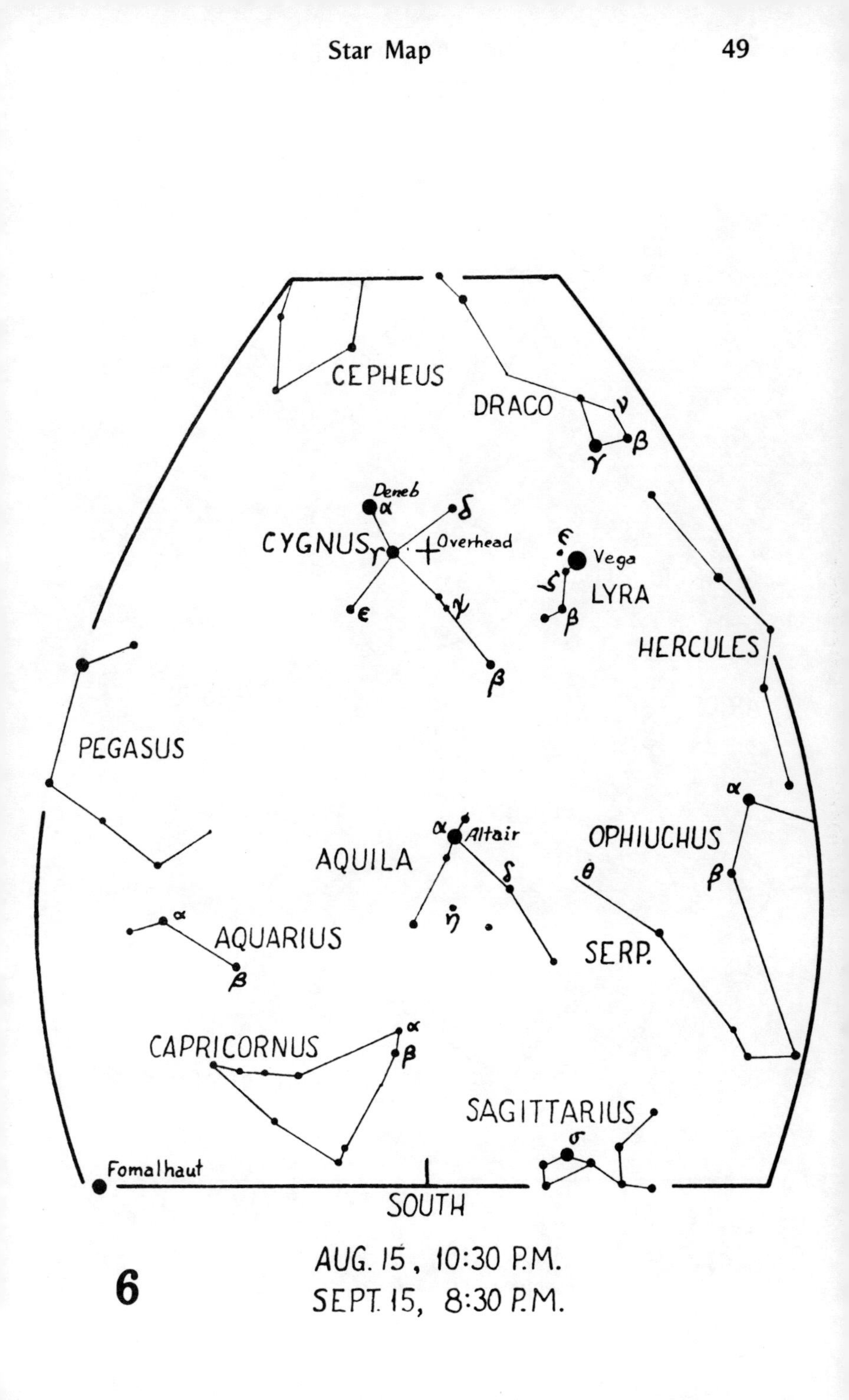

6

AUG. 15, 10:30 P.M.
SEPT. 15, 8:30 P.M.

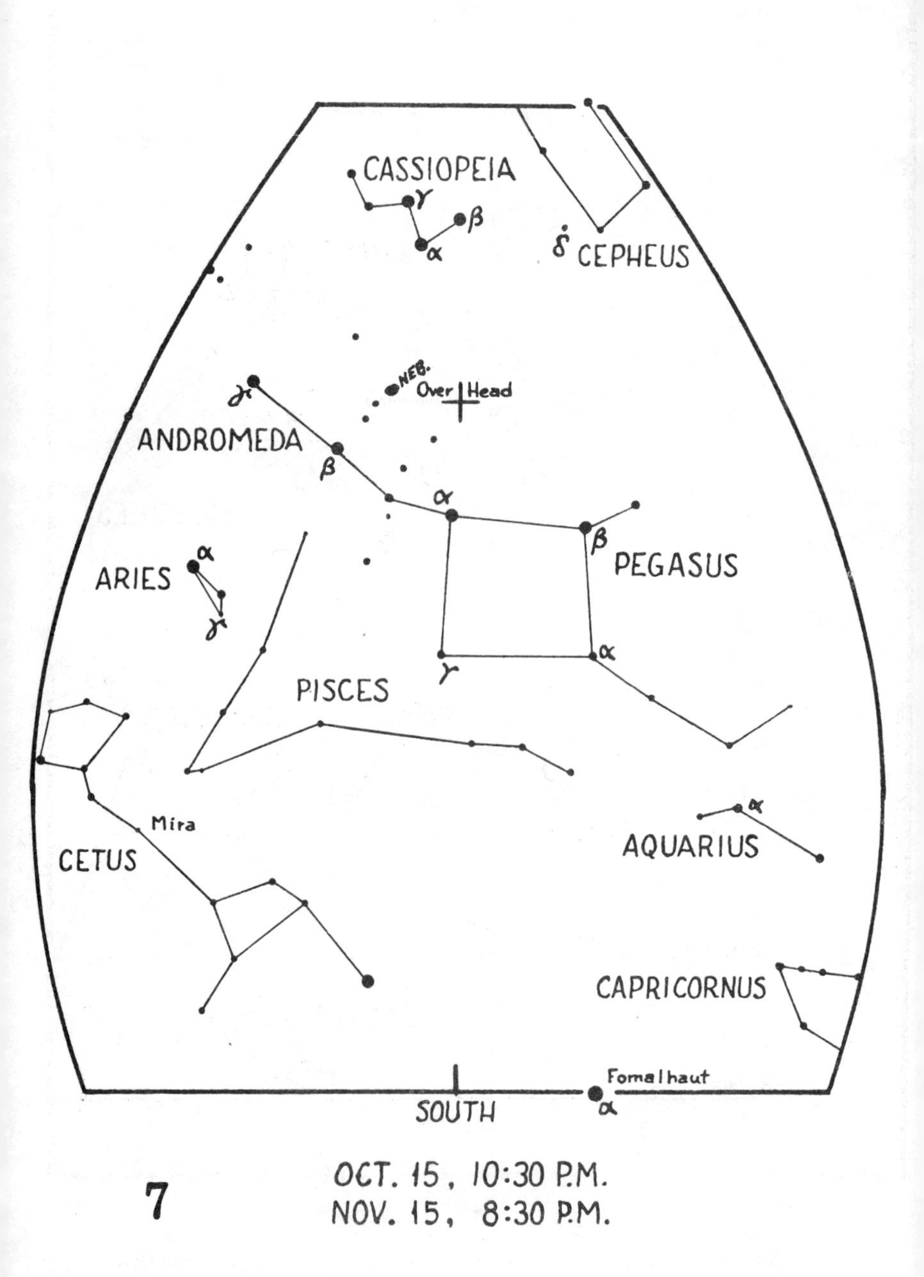

7

OCT. 15, 10:30 P.M.
NOV. 15, 8:30 P.M.

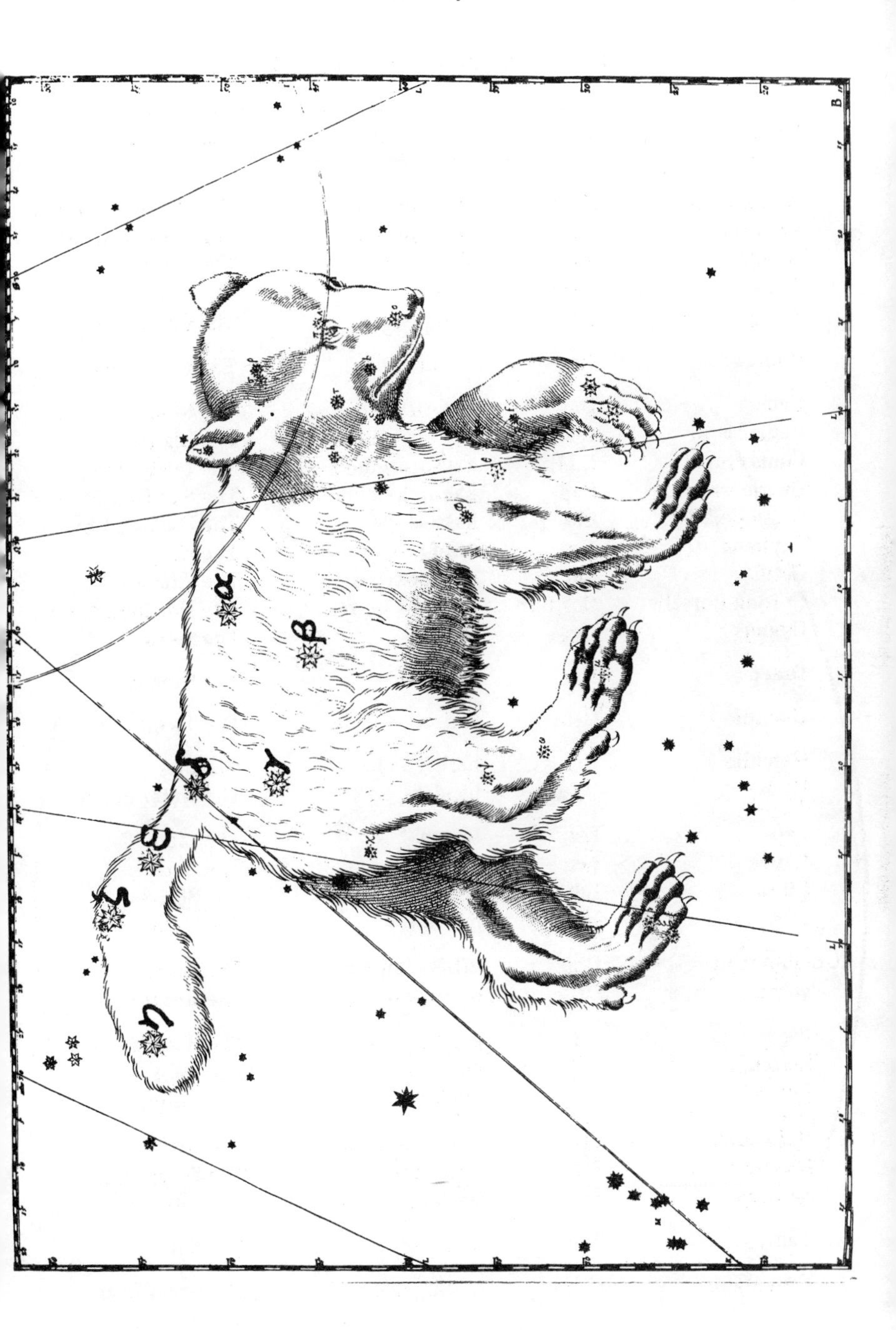

URSA MAJOR (from an old star atlas); note the seven stars comprising the "Big Dipper".

LIST OF MAJOR CONSTELLATIONS

Name	Abbr.	Pronunciation	Common Name
Andromeda	And	an-drom′-e-duh	The Chained Princess
Aquarius	Aqr	ak-ware′-euss	The Water Carrier
Aquila	Aql	ak′-wil-uh	The Eagle
Aries	Ari	a′-ri-ez	The Ram
Auriga	Aur	oh-rye′-guh	The Charioteer
Boötes	Boo	bo-oh′-tez	The Bear Driver
Cancer	Cnc	kan′-sir	The Crab
Canis Major	C Ma	kay′-niss major	The Big Dog
Canis Minor	C Mi	kay′-niss minor	The Little Dog
Capricornus	Cap	kap-rick-or′-nuss	The She Goat
Cassiopeia	Cas	kassi-ch-pe′-ya	The Queen's Chair
Cepheus	Cep	see′-fyooss	The King
Cetus	Cet	see′-tooss	The Whale
Corona Borealis	Cor Bor	kor-o′-na bo-re-al′-iss	The Northern Crown
Cygnus	Cyg	sig′-nuss	The Swan
Draco	Dra	dray′-ko	The Dragon
Gemini	Gem	jem′-ini	The Twins
Hercules	Her	herk′-yoo-leez	Hercules
Hydra	Hyd	hy′-dra	The Water Snake
Leo	Leo	lee′-oh	The Lion
Lepus	Lep	lee′-pus	The Hare
Libra	Lib	lye′-brah	The Scales
Lyra	Lyr	lye′-ruh	The Harp
Ophiuchus	Oph	off-ee-you′-cuss	The Serpent Holder
Orion	Ori	oh-rye′-on	The Hunter
Pegasus	Peg	peg′-uh-suss	The Winged Horse
Perseus	Per	per′-soos	The Hero
Pisces	Psc	pie′-seez	The Fishes
Sagittarius	Sgr	saj-it-tare′-euss	The Archer
Scorpius	Sco	skore′-pe-uss	The Scorpion
Serpens	Ser	sir′-penz	The Serpent
Taurus	Tau	taw′-russ	The Bull
Ursa Major	U Ma	er-suh′ major	The Great Bear (Great Dipper)
Virgo	Vir	ver′-go	The Virgin

NOTE: The following constellations do not appear on the maps in the interest of simplicity, since none are prominent.

LIST OF MINOR CONSTELLATIONS

Name	Abbr.	Pronunciation	Common Name
Camelopardalis	Cam.	ka-mel-opar′-duh-liss	Giraffe
Canes Venatici	C Vn	kay-neez ve-na′t-i-sye	Hunting Dogs
Coma Berenices	Com	ko-ma ber-e-ni′-seez	Berenice's Hair
Corvus	Crv	kor′-vuss	The Crow
Crater	Crt	kray′-ter	The Cup
Delphinus	Del	del′-fin-uss	The Dolphin
Equuleus	Equ	e-kwoo′-lee-uss	Little Horse
Eridanus	Eri	e-rid′-uh-nuss	River Eridanus
Lacerta	Lac	la-sert′-a	The Lizard
Leo Minor	L Mi	lee′-oh minor	Little Lion
Lynx	Lyn	links	Lynx
Monocerous	Mon	mo-noss′-er-ose	The Unicorn
Sagitta	Sge	sa-jit′-ta	The Arrow
Scutum	Sct	skoo′-tum	The Shield
Sextans	Sex	seks′-tanz	The Sextant
Triangulum	Tri	tri-ang′-u-lum	The Triangle
Vulpecula	Vul	vul-peck′-you-luh	The Little Fox

Chapter II
THE STELLAR SYSTEM

Now we are going to leave the individual stars, as well as their double, multiple and cluster, associations, and consider something immensely larger, our Stellar System. This has other names, including the Milky Way System, the Galactic System, and simply the Galaxy. Unlike the Solar System, which is made up simply of our Sun plus the various planets and moons, the Stellar System consists of literally millions of stars (or suns) all grouped together to form a titanic disc and spiral-shaped star system in space, with a more concentrated central nucleus (visible mainly in the Milky Way), and outer spiral arms, in one of which is located our Sun. This system, in turn, is only one of many such systems, or galaxies, scattered throughout space.

THE MILKY WAY

The Milky Way is a luminous, hazy band which encircles the entire visible heavens. Perhaps somewhat vaguely defined, some portions being more striking than others, its exact boundaries are difficult to determine. In the midwinter months the most prominent section is found in the Cassiopeia-Perseus-Auriga region, while the summer skies reveal far more striking portions, including the constellations of Cygnus, Ophiuchus, Sagittarius and Scorpio. Careful examinations with powerful field glasses or a small telescope show that this Milky Way is composed of thousands and even millions of faint stars, seemingly very closely crowded together (see plate 5 and Fig. 5 below). Indeed, in the Ophiuchus-Sagittarius region (see map 5 on page 48) the crowding is so marked as to earn the distinction of being termed "star clouds". The actual interpretation of this remarkable phenomenon is to be found in a later section. But let us now explore the region in detail.

Fig. 5: Left photo shows portion of constellation Cygnus in the Milky Way where stars are thick; right in Leo Minor where stars are thin. Photo courtesy of Lick Observatory.

GASEOUS NEBULAE

Here and there within the Milky Way we find curiously-shaped, vaguely shimmering objects which are not stars. They are termed "nebulae" (from the Latin, meaning mist or cloud) and are in many cases very striking and beautiful objects (plates 6 to 10). The use of the spectroscope reveals that they are composed largely of gasses, particularly oxygen, hydrogen, nitrogen, helium, neon and argon. Two types are recognized.

In one case, represented by a considerable diversity of forms, we find a close association of the nebula with a nearby very bright and very hot star. This star does not impart its light to the nebula by simple reflection, as is shown by the spectroscope. By some sort of flourescent process, which we do not completely understand, it causes the nebula to glow. We have agreed to classify such nebulae as "diffuse".

A second group are termed "planetary" because of their greenish, disk-like appearance being somewhat similar to the appearance of the planets Uranus or Neptune in a moderately powerful telescope (see plate 10). In the case of such planetary nebulae (about 500 are known) the greenish cast results from the presence of oxygen in unusual state, as shown by the spectroscope. Inside a planetary nebula is found a very hot central star, with a surface temperature of between 50,000° and 100,000° K (Absolute Temperature). These are the bluest known stars. The nebula itself probably represents an expanding spherical shell, which surrounds its associated central star and is again excited into luminescence.

DARK NEBULAE

The preceding two classes of nebulae are bright, due to the presence of an associated bright and very hot star, but what if such a star is absent? The answer is found in the large number of Milky Way objects which are dark and cut off the light of distant stars (see plate 9). There was a time in the history of astronomy when it was believed that certain dark spots or regions were "holes in the sky". Now we know better and can demonstrate the presence of large quantities of gas and dust in space.

In some cases this gas or dust makes its presence known by extreme contrasts, where one part of a photograph shows a rich field of stars and another on the same plate behaves as though a dark curtain had been drawn over it. In other cases we can demonstrate the existence of "cosmic dust" by the progressive reddening of the light of stars which passes through such dust-laden regions. Measures made seem to indicate that the particles involved are too small to stop or reflect the light backward, but that the light of the more distant stars of the Milky Way is progressively reddened and that the greater the distance, the greater is the reddening effect.

A rough analogy to this may be found in the reddening of the light of the setting Sun, due to passage of its light through the dust-laden Earth's atmosphere. Such "cosmic dust" is very wide-spread and, in some portions of space exists in very large amounts, although its distribution is far from uniform and its density is exceedingly low.

Still another form of space material is shown by the existence of gases in interstellar space. Such gases do not scatter the light as dust particles do; instead, they absorb it. The spectroscope has demonstrated the existence of very considerable amounts of hydrogen and calcium. Other elements are found in lesser quantities.

The presence of both gas and dust in space complicates all attempts to measure distance of considerable magnitude, such as tens of thousands of light years. Obscuration will produce a dimming and reddening of the light which is roughly proportional to the distance involved and the amount of the obscuring material through which the light must pass. Obviously, the fainter a certain star or star cluster appears, then the greater its distance from the observer, providing that interstellar gas and/or dust do not play a considerable part. But, if only a portion of the reduction in the light is due to distance and the remainder is caused by gas and/or dust, then the object may be considerably nearer than the total dimming effect indicates. Of course, if we have some other means of estimating the apparent reduction in brightness, then the amount due to obscuration may be computed. Unfortunately, it is far from constant; thus we immediately recognize the fact that the distribution of gas and dust in space is not uniform. This provides a considerable handicap in our attempts to explore our own immediate system of stars. Indeed, as has often been remarked, it is a striking fact that we know much more about the structure of neighboring external systems than we do about our own! The very large amounts of obscuring matter coupled with its non-uniform distribution obstructs our attempts to look out and handicaps our efforts to explore. In some cases we cannot look out at all, due to the presence of considerable amounts of obscuring material. As a result, any attempts to carefully delineate our stellar system must obviously be only approximate. In many ways this is quite unfortunate, but we have at least succeeded in attacking the problem in a number of ways and then putting the pieces together.

THE GALACTIC SYSTEM

The Milky Way, as we have now seen, comprises millions of stars, plus a considerable amount of associated gas and dust. The large majority of such stars must be at very considerable distances, because most of them are quite faint and are only found by the use of photography, employing very large telescopes. Indeed, it is estimated that the new 200 inch telescope at Mount Palomar has brought within our reach several billion stars which had never been seen before with the use of the 100 inch instrument at Mount Wilson.

The problem now before us is to synthesize this aggregation of stars, as well as other materials into some sort of system. Observations show us that without doubt the stars of the Milky Way are noticeably crowded, while in other portions of the celestial sphere the star density falls off rapidly by comparison (see Fig. 5 on page 54). Actually, when we are ninety degrees from the Milky Way, the number of stars per square degree in the sky has become a minimum. How may we rationalize what observations tell us of this phenomena? Is it not obvious that we are dealing here with a system of stars and that the Milky Way is of prime significance?

The answers to such questions have been given by the researchers of recent decades and all astronomers are convinced that all of the stars we can see and photograph (plus others we cannot yet reach) constitute a formidable system. We realize that the crowding of stars in the Milky Way is in itself significant, and that the exceptional crowding in the Sagittarius region (see map 5) also is more than mere "happenstance". The simple interpretation of the concentration of stars in the Milky Way is such that we are actually looking along and through the central plane of the system itself, where we see many more stars than at right angles to such a direction. In addition, the heavy concentration and greater total brightness of the Sagittarius region is simply explained by the realization that we are outside the system's center.

Putting this into others words, we may say that our stellar system is a flattened sort of structure, such that the extent of its major axis is a considerable multiple of the "thickness axis", perhaps on the order of 10 to 1. In order to visualize this we may resort to a number of crude analogies, such as a thick pancake, a watch case, or better yet, two dinner plates placed edge to edge facing each other. The Sun is not at the center and the greater brilliance in the Sagittarius region is an indication of this fact. The dimensions of this system are approximately 90,000 to 100,000 light years over all, with a "thickness" of about 5,000 to 8,000 light years. (See plate 12 for a galaxy similar to ours and with out-reaching arms like ours.)

The Sun is about two-thirds of the distance from the center toward the periphery, or about 30,000 light years. We believe it is in one of the arms of the spiral (such as appear in the Andromeda spiral in plate 11). The stars about it are not as thick as they are in the nucleus (found in Sagittarius).

The reader may well express wonder over the basis upon which this system has been established. He is likely to wonder more when he understands that we are unable to view the entire star aggregation, partially because we are a member of it ("you can't see the woods for the trees"), and partially because of the large amounts of obscuring material, which pervades so much of interstellar space and hampers our attempt at exploration.

Nevertheless, there are a number of pieces of evidence by which we are satisfied that the Galaxy is a vast system, embracing over 100 billion stars, plus associated clusters, nebulae, gas and dust. Listed on the next page are some of the basic reasons why we accept it.

(a) Suppose we had a photographic telescope which would show all the stars within a sky area of exactly one square degree, down to a certain limit of brightness, say star magnitude sixteen. In this manner we could obtain the number of stars per square degree in any part of the sky, except for the masking effects of interstellar gas and dust. However, we could avoid this drawback by the selection of areas wherein this effect was either minimized or lacking. If we make such counts, we would find that about 900 stars appear per square degree in the central regions of the Milky Way, about 270 stars 30° from the plane of the Milky Way, 120 stars at 60° and about 85 stars at 90°. These effects become even more pronounced when we include the even fainter stars below our limit of brightness. (See Fig. 5.)

The conclusion is simple. There is a very marked crowding of stars toward the main portions of the Milky Way, being on the order of about 10 to 1, compared with a direction at right angles to it.

According to this data, we must conclude that our stellar system has the general outline of a thin lens or disk. Since the region toward Sagittarius is the brighter portion of the Milky Way, then it follows that our Sun is not at the center of the system.

(b) Another basic way to study the extent of our stellar system is again undertaken by star counts. In this case we carefully count and tabulate the number of stars brighter than a certain magnitude, say the tenth, and suppose we find 320,000. Now we add the stars belonging to the tenth magnitude and obtain a grand total of 860,000 from which it is seen that 540,000 stars have been added and that the ratio of increase is 860,000/320,000 or 2.7 times. Since we have added 540,000 stars which are on the average far more distant, we would expect that the total volume of space involved would be greater and that we would naturally expect to get more stars. But the theoretical ratio is well-known from the simple solid geometry involved and is very nearly 1 to 4. This would argue that the stars do not continue to increase at a rate which remains constant as we go farther out into space. On the contrary, when we include the counts made from photographs, including very faint stars, the ratio is actually being reduced to about 1 to 1.5! The conclusion is inescapable: the stellar system is finite!

If we were to follow out the reasoning above, we could attempt to construct a "model" of the stellar system, but we may hasten to add that such a procedure would be quite erroneous because of the extra heavy concentration of stars in the Ophiuchus-Sagittarius portion, where their brightnesses have been seriously reduced because of the large amounts of gas and dust. This is confirmed in another way.

(c) During the last several decades tremendous strides have been taken in a new branch of astronomy which has been called "radio astronomy". By this means we can turn large radio telescopes, each shaped like an immense hollow disk, toward various portions of the heavens and record the results.

We find that the intensity of such radio radiations is very strong in the Milky Way and has a very strongly marked maximum toward the Sagittarius region.

(d) Careful investigations of the motions of the stars by the use of the spectroscope show that all stars are in motion, although the motions shown by many of them are quite difficult to detect. The sun's motion through space turns out to be about 12 miles a second, directed toward a point in the constellation of Hercules. Unfortunately, this is not all the story, for this velocity is merely that of the Sun relative to the stars (about 8,000 of them) which are its nearby neighbors. Suppose we now try to make such a comparison relative to stars far outside our immediate vicinity. This is not easily done, but we can piece together a number of different contributions.

The center of the Galaxy has already been indicated as in the general direction of Sagittarius and this has been confirmed by Shapley's work on the globular clusters, discussed below. We believe that all stars are in motion about this common center of gravity and that their motions are directly related to the distances from the center (nearest stars to it move fastest, the most distant move slowest).

While our conclusions must be considered as only provisional, we may state without serious contradiction that the Sun's distance from the center is about two-thirds of the distance to the outer edge, or close to 30,000 light years; and that, at this distance the Sun moves about the center with a speed which will require about 220 million years to complete the entire movement. During the time of the Earth's geologic history, as established by contemporary geologists, there have been over ten complete round trips of the Sun!

(e) Shapley's studies of the globular clusters include distance determinations, coupled with the fact that these objects show a very lopsided sky distribution. He was able to show that they are quite uniformly distributed with reference to the system center in Sagittarius. He was also able to show that they form a series of "suburban systems", grouped about the main one.

(f) Perhaps the clinching argument is to be found in the studies made of exterior systems (see Chapter III). These are spiral, elliptical and irregular external systems, many of whose distances are known. Even the nearest ones are well outside our own system.

(g) While the arrangement of material within our Galaxy constitutes still another problem, which is not easily solved because of our own position within the system, the use of radio astronomy has at least given a partial solution. By the use of radio telescopes we have been able to establish the presence of several arms of a spiral system (see plate 15). This is not at all unusual, since many such systems are known. They have a common structural characteristic: a central nucleus, surrounded by spiral arms, in which dust and gas and stars are found.

STELLAR EVOLUTION

Several decades ago astronomers had concluded, from an examination of the Russell Diagram (see page 23), that the life history of a star could be determined from the entries upon the chart. Supposedly a star started out relatively cool and reddish, gradually became hotter and bluer, reached a climax as a blue star, and then returned to a cool and inconspicuous "old age" as a red star once more, finally to become cold and unseen as a member of the senile ("dead") star group.

Since that time we have re-examined the question of a star's history and have come up with a somewhat different approach and different results. This has been a consequence of some very remarkable changes in the knowledge of astrophysics. We have good reasons for believing that stars are created. The main question is how they are created, their source of energy and their behavior during their life cycle. Naturally, this is one of the most highly speculative portions of modern astronomy and all present day conclusions are to be considered only as tentative. New discoveries may at any moment entirely revise our theories once again.

We still maintain that stars are born, that they mature and that they finally die from the complete consumption of their internal energy. At the same time we have modified our theories in accord with two relatively new and very important discoveries:

(a) The source of all stellar energy, including that of our Sun, is atomic energy. Certain atomic reactions (and there are several possible kinds) are responsible for the continuous flow of energy which stars radiate. In the case of a nova (see page 30) this normal reaction is hurried up to the point where an atomic explosion takes place. In the case of certain variable stars the process is modified at intervals.

(b) Evidence has been accumulated in large quantities to show that in our own Galaxy and other neighboring stellar systems the hottest and brightest stars are always found in regions which contain large amounts of gas and dust.

It is not too difficult to postulate the "life" of a star. The earth is said by geologists to be some 4½ billion years old and its past history has been one of rather wide-spread and catastrophic change. There are several hypotheses regarding its creation along with the rest of the solar system.

In developing the life history of a star we find that the most difficult part is the beginning. As before mentioned, we believe that the widespread cosmic dust and clouds are the basic materials. Some astronomers maintain that certain congestive "globules" seen in photographs of portions of the Milky Way are indeed "embryonic stars". Perhaps we must be content with this, as modern astronomy is less than a century old! It will take many centuries of patient photography to give us some clues of changes indicating a process at work! So, for purpose of argument, let us suppose we have an extremely young star. It will be very hot through contraction, and it continues contracting as it moves into the left hand portion of the Hertzsprung-Russell Diagram (page 23). The very hot ones will be class B if they are very massive, since they are able to contract most rapidly; the less massive will arrive in the yellow to reddish portions. The hot inner cores are now ready to initiate the atomic process of change of hydrogen into helium. Thus there is little change in the stars at this stage of the game. When the core hydrogen is nearly used up, things begin to happen!

Over many billions of years the star may have grown over 200 times as large in diameter with a corresponding reduction in density; it is now a red giant. Here it can go in any one of three different paths:

(a) If the interior of the red giant is consumed, accompanied with shrinkage to the size of the earth with enormous density, it becomes a white dwarf (the small companion of Sirius is a good example). This assumes that it remains stable.

(b) If it is unstable it may explode and become a neutron star, 100 million times as dense as the white dwarf.

(c) If it contracts to the size of the neutron star, but does not stabilize, the entire body through compression collapses and becomes a "black hole", which has such strong gravitation that no energy may escape from it. Note: to find a black hole is similar to finding a black hat in a dark room! Fortunately, there are a number of double stars (two stars moving about their common center of gravity like Sirius) where the companion star is invisible!

Do not be disturbed by the impact of the above information. The Sun has a long life ahead of it and long before any violent change takes place it will have become too hot to support life on this earth!

The above brief outline is what we may call current working hypothesis; but an hypothesis is a temporary thing and its great advantage is that it may be modified with the coming of new discoveries.

CONCLUSION

What does our Galaxy really look like? We can only turn to the appearances of other systems for a clue, since we are so much within our own system and cannot see it as it might be seen from the outside. A good guess is that it looks like the common spiral form when looked down upon (see plate 11) and when seen "edgewise" on (plate 13). With this we must be content.

Unfortunately, our explorations are limited to one portion of our galactic system because of the impossibility of penetrating the heavy dust clouds in the Sagittarius region. This is a matter of disappointment, even of frustration, for we actually know much more and in greater detail about our nearer neighboring systems than we do about our own! We will now focus our attention upon these exterior systems (galaxies), which exist in very large numbers.

Plate 11: *THE ANDROMEDA SPIRAL NEBULA,* M. 31. A galaxy of millions of stars very similar to our own galaxy. Photograph courtesy of Lick Observatory.

Chapter III
GALAXIES AND OUTER SPACE

Note to the reader: there are so many nebulae and clusters that it has become necessary to name them by the use of:

(a) Messier's List, compiled near the close of the 18th century, and utilizing the capital letter M coupled with a number of the object in his list; example: M. 33, the spiral nebula in Triangulum.

(b) The New General Catalog and the Index Catalog, both being relatively modern. Examples: NGC 6822 and IC 1613.

(c) The number in the list of a certain observatory, when the object is not in the previous catalogs.

Introduction

It is indeed an unfortunate circumstance, bound up with the history of astronomy, which forces us to use word "nebula" as a general term. Originally it was applied to any indistinct astronomical object which presented a rather vague and indefinite outline, as seen in the telescopes of the past. Such visual observation has largely been replaced by photography, which permits us to see more, due to the additive effect that light has upon the plate emulsion. Another advantage is that we obtain a permanent record.

In the meantime we have learned to distinguish between diffuse and planetary nebulae on the one hand (which are definitely a part of our own galactic system) and, on the other hand, a very large group of interesting and, in many ways, remarkable objects known as "exterior galaxies" or spiral nebulae. We may add that not all of such systems are spiral in appearance, some being elliptical and others quite irregular.

Aside from the startling realization that a considerable number of these exterior systems encompass and indicate a much larger total physical universe, we are faced with a formidable task in observing, classifying and interpreting these objects. Let us trace the history of this subject during the current century.

THE ANDROMEDA PROBLEM

This problem arose in connection with the fact that the brightest (though barely visible to the naked eye) and apparently the largest of its class of spiral nebulae (Andromeda Nebula, see plate 11) had resisted all efforts in distance determination. Furthermore, the spectroscope showed none of the characteristics of an ordinary diffuse nebula, giving instead an integrated dark line spectrum ordinarily associated only with stars.

The outbreak of a nova within this object in the year 1885 made it quite apparent that the Andromeda spiral nebula was at an immense distance, since the nova was of the seventh magnitude (apparent) and about a tenth the total brightness of the entire nebula itself. Assuming it to be an ordinary nova, its absolute magnitude would have been minus seven and the great spiral would thus have been at a distance measured in tens or even hundreds of thousands of light years, which astronomers of that day were quite unwilling to accept. Since that time our knowledge of novae has improved by leaps and bounds and we now know that this was a supernova, whose absolute magnitude was close to minus sixteen and a distance figure measured in hundreds of thousands of light years! If it had been close in our own galaxy, it would have been the most brilliant object in our entire night sky!

Shortly after the turn of the twentieth century astronomers were divided into two camps. The smaller group believed that the Andromeda and other spiral nebulae were actually external systems, similar perhaps to our own Galaxy and they pointed to the stellar characteristics of its spectrum to support this contention. The other group contended that such exterior systems were quite impossible because this would entail a total universe composed of large numbers of universe units and would involve overall distances which would be unthinkable. It is interesting to note that man has always resisted efforts to expand the physical world, which would reduce proportionally his place within it! Let us now see which group proved to be right.

The controversy noted above continued during the early decades of the present century. Finally it was resolved by Edwin Hubble, a young astronomer at the Mount Wilson Observatory, where the largest telescope then available had been put into use. He decided that long and careful exposures of the Andromeda spiral, especially of the outer regions, might conceivably resolve such selected portions into individual stars. By 1923 he had succeeded in this undertaking. He showed that the Andromeda spiral nebula was indeed an external system, containing stars, star clusters, diffuse nebulae, gas, dust and Cepheids. Indeed, it was by the use of these Cepheids that Hubble announced a distance for the object of about three-quarters of a million light years! This was subject to uncertainty because of the difficulty in properly allowing for the absorption of the light by intervening dust.

The central portion of the spiral stubbornly refused all attempts to resolve its structure until Baade in 1943 did this successfully by the use of red-sensitive plates and showed that the central portion is composed of stars whose brightest members are red, while the brightest stars in the arms are blue. The former are now called Population II, the latter Population I.

Baade and others were able to show the existence of two classes of Cepheids, one associated with Population I stars (Type I Cepheid Variables) and the other with Population II stars (Type II Cepheids). This required a revision of the distance figure and it was set at 1,500,000 light years. In other words, the light we have received upon our recent plates started before man had even become civilized! The implications of such facts are obvious, and are astonishing when given serious consideration.

It had now become evident that a new and startling concept of the physical universe was required, such that it must be composed of many unit universes, each complete in itself. This was the immediate consequence of the fact that if the Andromeda spiral was an external system, then all the others of like nature (and hundreds were known at that time) must also be individual external systems. Catalogs of such objects had been made as far back as the time of the Herschels, but Dreyer's "New General Catalog", later followed by the First and Second "Index Catalogs", listed over ten thousand of such objects. Continuation of this work by the use of photography has greatly extended our lists. It is estimated that the 200 inch telescope can reach all galaxies up to a limiting distance of approximately 2 million light years, and we are startled with the realization that 10 billion or more galaxies are now within our reach!

THE LOCAL GROUP

Ever since the proof of the nature of the Andromeda spiral and the calculation of its distance we have naturally been interested in the existence of other relatively near neighbors to our own Galaxy. This has meant the careful scrutiny of many photographs, coupled with the attempts to calculate distances by the use of Cepheids or other means. Having done so, we are now in a position to enumerate those systems which may at present be classified as our "neighbors" at a distance. In addition, if we know how big an object appears and have its approximate distance, then we are able to obtain its actual size. We are rather surprised to find that some of the neighboring systems are not spirals. Indeed, it has recently become evident that other forms also exist in considerable quantity.

Table 5 (shown on next page) includes those systems which are, at this writing, included in the "Local Group". Not including our own Galaxy, they make up a total of thirteen such systems. The name of the system, coupled with its approximate distance, is followed by comments, and the estimate of size in parentheses is included.

We may remark that this table does not show a preponderance of any type of structure and that their distribution in space is not uniform. Indeed, our Galaxy plus the Magellanic Clouds (see plate 14), and the Sculptor and Fornax systems all lie within a space of a half million light years.

The three spirals included in the group are very large, in comparison to other spirals. The remaining systems have a somewhat smaller range in size than comparable systems known elsewhere. Furthermore, members of the group may conceivably be hidden from view by the dust clouds of the Milky Way itself.

TABLE V: THE LOCAL GROUP

1. **The Galaxy**: distance 0; probably spiral (70,000 light years).
2. **Andromeda** (M. 31): distance 1,500,000 light years; large spiral, tilted at an angle of about 15 degrees; bright nucleus and numerous arms; has star clusters, globular clusters, Cepheids, novae, diffuse nebulae, obscuring material; brightest stars of absolute magnitude -7 or -8; (85,000 l. y. in diameter). See plate 11 on page 63.
3. **Triangulum** (M. 33): distance 1,550,000 l. y.; a beautiful, loosely constructed spiral of symmetrical shape; bright nucleus and some obscuring material; clusters and bright nebulae; novae and Cepheids; evidence of some rotation; (30,000 l. y.). See plate 12 on page 73.
4. **Large Magellanic Cloud**: distance 140,000 l.y.; easily observed by the naked eye from stations in the southern hemisphere (Plate 14); irregular appearance; dust, gas, bright nebulosity, blue and red supergiant stars, several thousand Cepheids, much ionized hydrogen gas; most Population I, but small amount of Population II objects (30,000 l.y.).
5. **Small Magellanic Cloud**: 160,000 l. y.; similar to preceding, but smaller and almost free of obscuring dust; richer in Population II stars and materials than is the LMC (above), but smaller amounts of hydrogen nebulae; (24,000 l.y.).
6. **Messier 32** (in Andromeda); 1,500,000 l.y.; elliptical; (5,000 l. y.). See notes below.
7. **NGC 205** (in Andromeda); 1,500,000 l. y.; elliptical (9,000 l. y.). See notes below.
8. **IC 1613**: 1,400,000 l. y.; irregular; contains nebulous material and Cepheids; (9,000 l. y.).
9. **NGC 6822**: 1,000,000 l. y.; irregular; (6,000 l. y.).
10. **NGC 185**: 1,300,000 l. y.; elliptical; (5,500 l. y.).
11. **NGC 147**: 1,300,000 l. y.; elliptical (5,500 l. y.).
12. **Fornax system**: 450,000 l. y.; elliptical (6,500 l. y.).
13. **Sculptor system**: 200,000 l. y.; elliptical (3,500 l. y.).
14. **Wolf-Lundmark system**: 500,000 l. y.; irregular (6,000 l. y.).

NOTE: Several more systems are not yet included in this Local Group, pending further information. In addition later determinations indicate that some of the distances must be revised and are actually greater!

The absolute magnitudes of the members of the local group range from -19.6 for the Andromeda spiral to -10.6, and such luminosities are probably typical.

Observations by photography indicate the presence of considerable amounts of gas and dust, which are often detected by the dimming and reddening effect on stars beyond them. Gaseous regions often are spotted by their brightness and checks of their spectra. One fact stands out from examination of the irregular and spiral systems by photography. This is the presence of rather large amounts of gas and dust, whereas all such gas and dust seems to be conspicuous by its absence in the elliptical systems and in the central regions of spiral galaxies.

OTHER GALAXIES

Other galaxies are known in considerable quantity, but all may be classified in structural appearance in one of the following categories:

(a) **Irregular.** These, as the class name indicates, do not yield any special form, being composed of a heterogeneous aggregation of stars and dust. Symbol I is the letter symbol of the class. (See plate 14, page 75.)

(b) **Elliptical.** This form is spherical or somewhat flattened, the degree of flattening or ellipticity being shown by a number coupled with the symbol E. These begin with EO (spherical) and proceed in order, E1, E2, E3, E4, E5, E6, and E7, the highest so far discovered (see plate 17, page 78).

(c) **Spiral**, divided into two sub-headings. The **normal spirals** (symbol S) are characterized by a uniform nucleus, to which spiral arms are attached. All are relatively thin and flat and they are tipped toward us at all possible angles, ranging from full plane views (90 degrees) to edgewise (0 degrees). (See plates 11, 12, 13, 15, and 18). See plate 19 for barred spiral.

The **barred spirals** (SB) are similar to the normal type, except that the arms are attached to the ends of a central bar, rather than to a round central nucleus. Both of the above subclasses seem to come in a wide variety of forms, differing among themselves in the amount of material in the arms and the degree of prominence of the arms relative to the central nucleus. We attach the letters a, b, or c to the symbol to show this, so that the great Andromeda system becomes Sb and a system which is mostly arms is Sc.

At one time it was thought that the spirals were far greater in numbers than the other two classes, but later investigations cast considerable doubt upon such a conclusion. Some authorities go even farther and insist that all three basic forms are related through an orderly evolutionary process, beginning with the I (irregular), running through the S (spiral), and terminating with the E (elliptical). However, such an explanation may be premature at the present state of our knowledge, although the differences in content of Population I and Population II stars versus the presence or absence of dust in the elliptical nebulae would tempt one into such an obvious interpretation.

DISTANCE

Distance determinations for external stellar systems are made by one or more of the following methods (sometimes more than one at a time will be employed to serve as a check):

(a) **Cepheids.** These we know to be luminous giant stars, whose range of absolute magnitudes are well known. Very useful are these for obtaining the distances of the nearer systems, for which Cepheid identification is relatively easily obtained. (See the section on Variable Stars starting on page 27.)

(b) Novae. While novae (or suddenly brilliant stars) are not common, and supernovae are relatively uncommon, our knowledge of these unusual stars furnishes us with a powerful tool in obtaining distances. Furthermore, if and when such a nova or supernova is discovered, it will furnish a valuable check on the distance value as determined by another method.

(c) **Brightest star.** This method is often employed when the preceding ones are not able to be used, but where it is possible to measure the apparent magnitude of the brightest star in a given external system. Since we can assign a reasonable absolute magnitude to such a star, based upon our total experience, the determination of distance follows immediately. This is done by a complex equation too complicated to explain in a beginning book.

(d) **Absolute magnitudes of galaxies** may be obtained by photography of the more distant systems and comparing the apparent magnitudes with those of objects already known. Once we are able to calibrate such determinations properly, the distance figures follow immediately. While distance so obtained may be subject to considerable error in some cases, it is usually quite reliable.

(e) **Apparent diameters of galaxies,** as obtained on a photographic plate, should be inversely proportional to distance, provided that all are of about the same linear diameter. Unfortunately, there seems to be a rather considerable range of diameters of various systems, although the use of an average figure will thus give us a rough approximation to distance if all other methods have failed.

ROTATION

Rotation has been demonstrated in several external systems, perhaps the best known being the great Andromeda spiral, whose central regions seem to rotate as a solid body (even though they are not one), but at greater distances from the center the rotational velocity decreases, just as it does for the outer planets of our solar system. In addition we have already seen that the motion of the Sun about the central portions of our own Galaxy is well established, so that our own system also exhibits rotational characteristics.

CLUSTERING

Clustering of galaxies seems to be quite common, our own system being a member of a small group of systems. The general picture seems to be that of fairly uniform distribution in space, but groupings of at least several dozen clusters of galaxies have been recognized. The nearest known cluster to our own group is one located in the constellation of Virgo and distant approximately 40 million light years! Further photographic research may shed additional light on this very puzzling phase of modern astronomy.

GALAXY STARS

Galaxy stars seemingly differ somewhat in make-up in various situations. The arms of spirals and the irregular galaxies are characterized by a stellar population in which the brighter stars are blue giants, along with considerable amounts of gas and dust. In other words, this is a Population I make-up. (See page 61 and 62 for an explanation of the life history of a star.)

On the other hand, the central portions of the spirals contain stars whose brightest members are red giants, and such a Population II region is relatively quite transparent. The elliptical galaxies, with their exclusively Population II membership do not differ markedly from the spiral nuclei.

It is tempting, therefore, to suppose that, as the spiral arms become more tightly coiled about the nucleus and their Population I becomes Population II through an evolutionary aging process, that such spiral systems may be transformed into elliptic systems. However, we must add that such changes would occupy billions of years and it may be quite premature to suggest them at the present state of our knowledge. We may well be accused here of undue haste when we recollect that in a dense cluster of galaxies the chances of a "merger collision" are reasonably good, due to mutual tidal action. If so, interstellar gases may well be "swept up" and consolidated or even ejected, thus freeing the system of such debris and producing a member galaxy which is entirely devoid of gas and dust material. Several such members of the Coma Berenices cluster are well known.

Radio astronomy has shown a strong source in the constellation Cygnus and photographs made with the 200 inch telescope at Mt. Palomar immediately disclosed a rich cluster of galaxies in that direction. The radio source seems to have two close condensation points, which have been concluded to be the centers of radio radiation of two colliding galaxies. One troublesome fact, still unexplained, is that in this radio region the total radiation is far in excess of the amount we would expect. Further work may resolve the difficulty.

THE RED SHIFT

After the discovery of large numbers of external systems (galaxies), the next obvious step was to test them for Doppler shift in their spectra. We may be reminded at this point that the Doppler Principle, when employed upon any objects which are not moving at right angles to the observer, simply indicates a motion toward the observer if the entire spectrum is shifted to the blue end and a corresponding motion away from the observer where the spectrum is shifted to the red (see page 26). In addition, the magnitude of its velocity is proportional to the amount of the measured shift.

Astronomers at Mount Wilson (particularly Hubble, Humason, and Mayall) calculated the Doppler shifts on a considerable number of external systems. Although there are a number of difficulties, particularly in the assignment of proper distances to the more distant galaxies, there were two important conclusions reached by these researches:

(a) The red shift relationship does not appear to hold for the local group.

(b) For others there is a simple linear relationship: the amount of shift is directly proportional to the distance of the individual galaxy or, in other words, the greater the distance of an individual galaxy, the greater is the velocity of the recession from our system!

As an example of the red shift relationship, we may cite the figures for a given pair of galaxies as follows:

NGC 221 has a measured shift of 125 miles per second and a distance of 1.5 million light years, while NGC 4473 has the equivalent figures at 1400 miles per second and 16 million light years. The approximate 1:10 proportion is quite evident, although we must remember that it cannot be exact because of the inherent errors in obtaining such large distances.

What is the meaning of this astonishing relationship? We are faced with a choice between two alternatives: (1) the red shift is not a true shift at all, OR (2) it is a true shift. Each will then require some satisfactory explanation. Let us examine these alternatives.

(1) The easiest way out of our dilemma is to suppose that the red shift is not a true shift and that something happens to the light itself en route from the distant galaxy to the observer, so that it is reddened. Besides, such a loss of energy would be proportional to the distances involved, which is in accordance with what we observe.

Unfortunately, we are faced here with an impasse, since we cannot (at least so far) duplicate this unknown process in the laboratory. Another way of stating this is to say that outer space is our laboratory and we are quite ignorant of what has presumably happened to the light in traversing outer space! So our attempt to discredit the red shift on the basis of "tired light" brings us up against a stone wall.

(2) The other alternative is to accept the red shift as real, which will immediately remind us that if the more distant systems are moving faster,

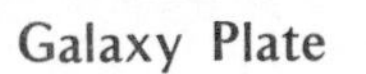

Plate 12: *THE SPIRAL NEBULA* in TRIANGULUM, M. 33. This is another stellar system like our own. Photograph courtesy of Lick Observatory.

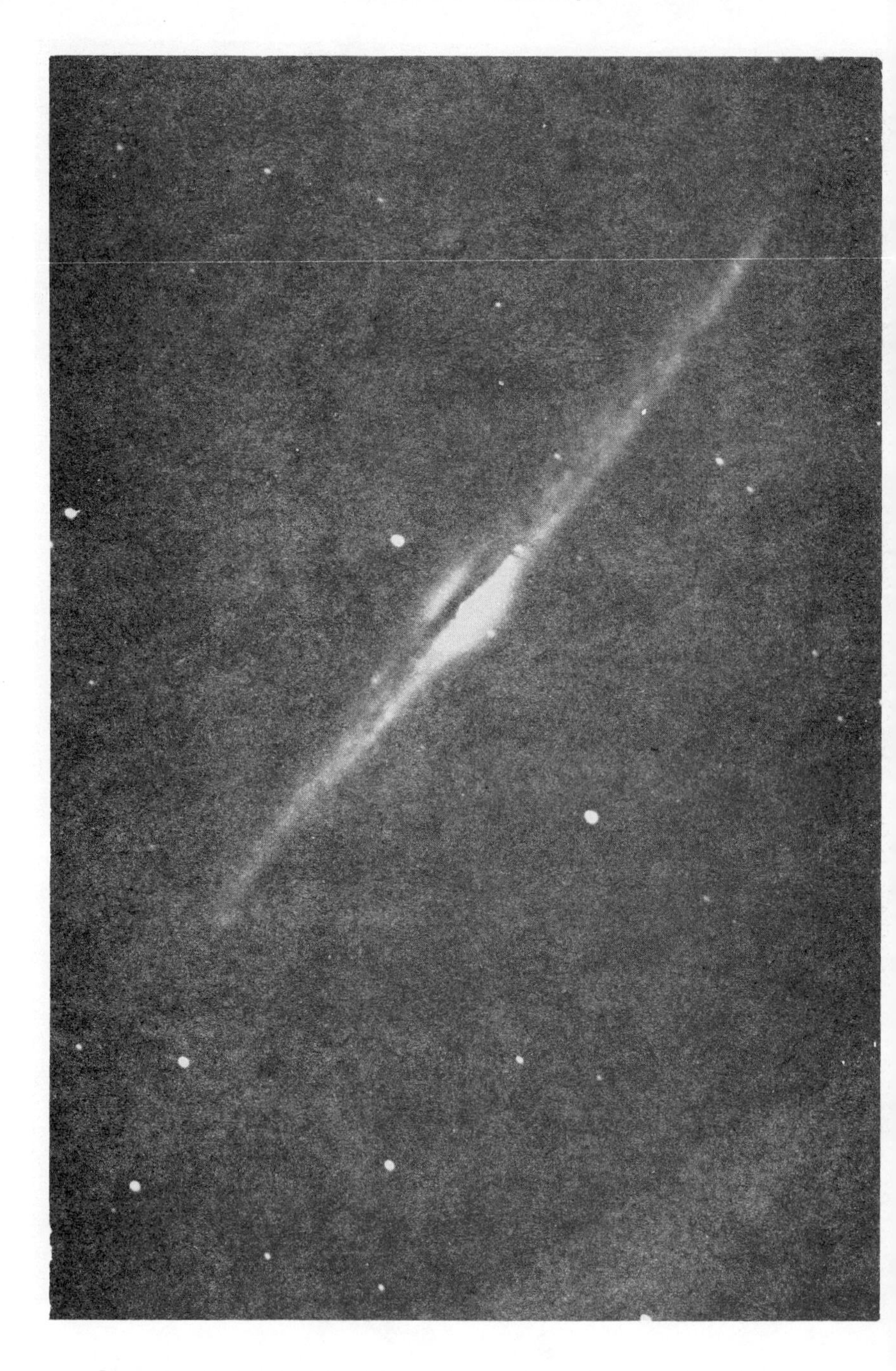

Plate 13: *AN EDGEWISE SPIRAL NEBULA* in COMA BERENICES (east of ARCTURUS in Star Map 4). Photograph courtesy of Lick Observatory.

Plate 14: *THE LARGE MAGELLANIC CLOUD.* Seen in the southern and tropic parts of the world only; might be called a satellite stellar system of our own Milky Way Galaxy because of being so close to it. Photograph courtesy of the Lick Observatory.

Plate 15: *NGC 5364 SPIRAL GALAXY* in VIRGO. Photograph courtesy of Hale Observatories.

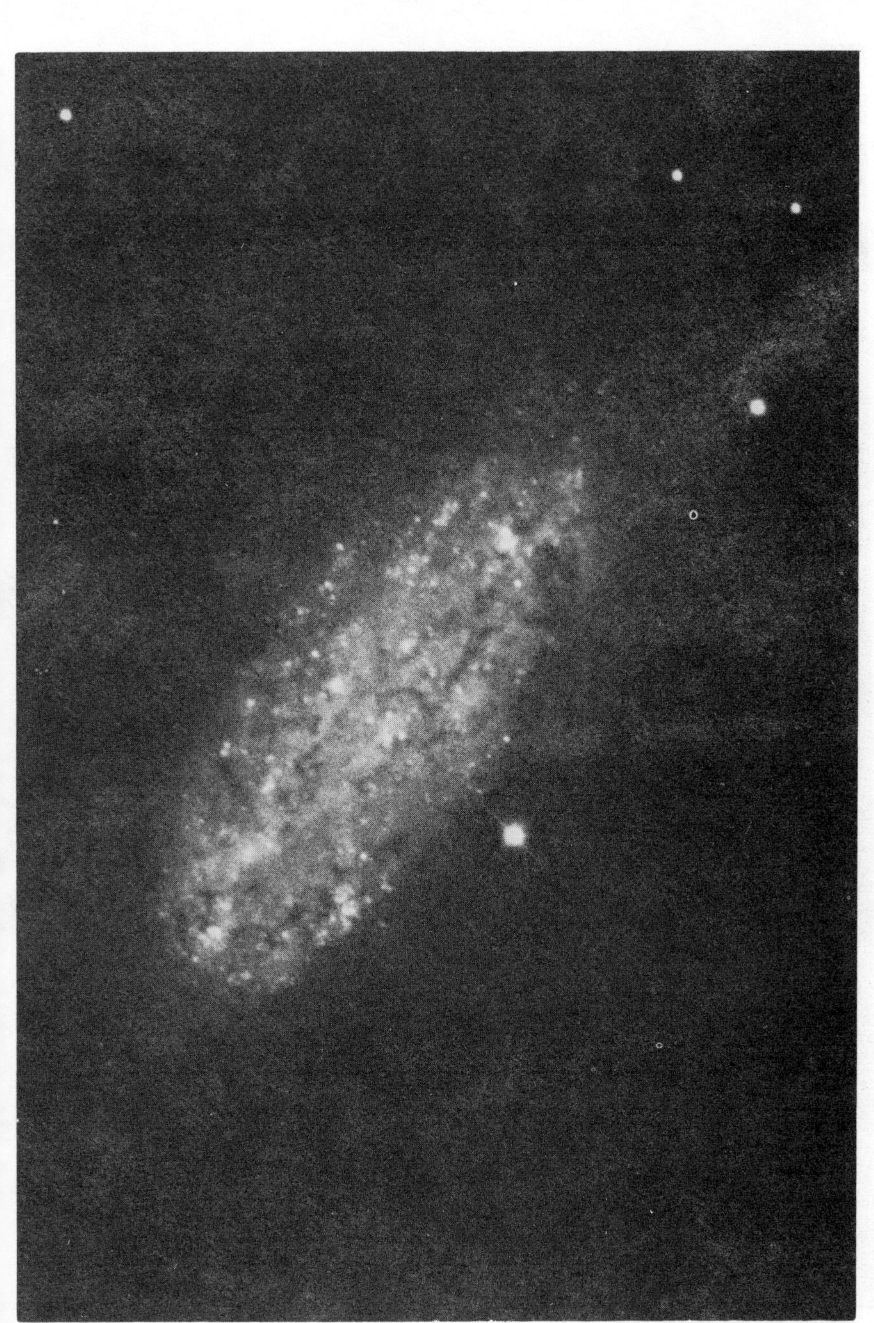

Plate 16: *THE ELLIPTICAL NEBULA,* NGC 2976. Photograph courtesy of Lick Observatory.

Plate 17: *ELLIPTICAL NEBULA* in VIRGO, M. 87. Photograph courtesy of Lick Observatory.

Plate 18: *NGC 5194 SPIRAL GALAXY* in CANES VENATICI, Messier 51. SATELLITE GALAXY is NGC 5195. Photograph courtesy of Hale Observatories.

Plate 19: *NGC 1300 BARRED SPIRAL GALAXY* in ERIDANUS. Photograph courtesy of Hale Observatories.

then we are in a sort of universe which is in a state of expansion and all of its members are increasing their distances from one another! Consider a balloon with a particle at its center and several other particles around the outer portions of the space inside. If the balloon is expanded by blowing it larger with more gas, then all such particles will be farther removed from the central particle and also from one another.

This second alternative has led to another question, which is: What is the nature of space? Let us attempt to show that space may indeed have a variety of characteristics and that these are bound to be considered as part of the problem.

THE PROBLEMS OF OUTER SPACE

The problems of outer space are entirely out of the range of human experience because they involve abstractions, the concepts of which are entirely removed from human experience. Let us introduce this world of the abstract by poising a very simple question, which is: Granting that the Red Shift is true and at the same time supposing that our telescopic improvements would in time be sufficient to reach galaxies which are receding at a speed greater than the speed of light; then, would such galaxies be visible at all when they are moving away from the observer faster than the light they give out?

Newtonian physics teaches us that the light sent out from a galaxy under such circumstances would never reach the Earth. Are such concepts reasonable? Do we live in a truly Newtonian Universe? One physicist of the current century thought not, and his theories upset the entire scientific world. Indeed, his findings have forced us to revise the basic concepts of physical science for the current century.

When Albert Einstein was 26 years old, he proposed the Special Theory of Relativity, which presented an entirely new concept. He argued that in space a fixed framework does not exist; that the velocity of light is constant everywhere and cannot be increased by the motion of its source or the motion of the observer. Therefore, nothing in the total universe can travel faster than the speed of light.

Einstein then formulated a series of equations, now a basic portion of modern physics. The all important thing is that his equations make all distance and time measures depend upon the velocity of the observer! Suppose two galaxies are on opposite sides from the Earth and each recedes at a speed of three-fourths the speed of light. Does this mean that they are each moving away from the other at six-fourths of three halves the speed of light? Nonsense, says Einstein! Observers in both galaxies would each take their own time and distance measures, and these would be entirely different from those made by observers here on the Earth. Their combined velocities must turn out to be somewhat less than the velocity of light.

Relativity has been repeatedly verified by certain delicate tests, among the simplest being the bending of light, which comes from a star and passes close to the Sun's gravitational field, which causes it to slightly bend. In addition, relativity teaches us that there is no such thing as an "absolute" or fixed series of measurements, since all such measures depend upon the location of the observer and he can never be entirely certain that the measurements he makes in the depths of outer space are reliable!

Coupled with relativity concepts we must also introduce the question of space geometry in order to obtain a satisfactory concept of the nature of the total universe. We are used to Euclidian geometry, therefore we always assume as fact the basic axioms that the straight line is the shortest distance between two points and the sum of the angles of a triangle becomes 180 degrees, and we may argue that this is quite sufficient.

So it is, for our own restricted pursuits, but navigators have shown that on the spherical surface of the Earth itself the shortest distance between two points is the "great circle" through these two points. Einstein brought forward a new concept and stated that the nature of the total universe depended upon the nature of space itself, for who is to say authoritatively that it must be Euclidian space? He showed that the presence of any body possessing gravitational properties would warp the region of space surrounding it, so that one could not simply assume that space is Euclidian. It may not be so.

Theorists now see three possibilities as to the nature of outer space, and each represents a certain kind of total universe. They are as follows:

(a) **Euclidian space** has no curvature. The straight line distance between two points is the shortest distance and the sum of the angles of a triangle is 180°. Einstein rejected this because of the part played by the gravitational field. We may note that such a Euclidian universe would be infinite.

(b) **Positively curved space is similar to a sphere,** where the shortest distance between two points is their "great circle" (like the meridians of the Earth) and the sum of the angles of a triangle is greater than 180°. This forms a finite but extremely vast system. The earth itself is a fair sample, since a straight line over its surface eventually returns to the same place.

(c) **Negatively curved or saddle-shaped space.** In this universe the shortest distance between two points would be their open curve (parabola or hyperbola) and the sum of the angles of a triangle is less than 180°. Such a system would be infinite.

Which of these three views is right? Only time will tell, since it will take many more years of measurement to settle the question. Some time ago we thought that the proof of a negatively curved and infinite space was assured, but now there is some doubt of this and perhaps the positively curved and finite system may yet win out.

COSMOLOGY

Cosmology means the study of the universe as an orderly system or cosmos. Over a hundred years ago the eminent German scientist Alexander von Humboldt published an ambitious survey of the entire physical world, entitled "Kosmos". Today such a task would prove quite impossible for one man, so immense has become our storehouse of scientific knowledge of the physical world. The astronomers themselves have made observations of the make-up of the universe which have proven to be as amazing in their scope as the facts themselves.

Such giant telescopes as the 200 inch at Mount Palomar, coupled with numerous radio telescopes distributed throughout the world, have plumbed the depths of space to an extent heretofore never considered possible. Data now assembled indicate that we now have a total universe whose main constituents are galaxies and clusters of such galaxies, while each of these components is in itself a vast system of member stars, gas and dust.

It is only natural that the interpretation of these astronomical facts should be undertaken by someone. As a result we have a branch of physical science called "cosmology", which treats the universe as an orderly system. It is the duty of the cosmologist to complement the work of the observer and to produce as close a coordination with the latter as is possible.

The cosmologist is strictly a theorist and it is his job to set up "models" of the total universe which are reasonable in the light of observational data, coupled with the present status of astrophysics. Such models have been constructed even by the philosophers of ancient times. Plato, Aristotle, Lucretius, and Ptolemy among others speculated upon the nature of the universe, which in their time was exceedingly restricted. In the Middle Ages such men as Bruno, Copernicus, Galileo and Kepler played their parts, while in later times Newton, Huygens, Kant, Wright and Herschel contributed. In the later decades of the current century we must list such illustrious names as Einstein, Hubble, De Sitter, Le Maitre, Eddington, Milne, Gamow, Bondi and Hoyle, to name a few.

It is from the work of this last group that we obtain our cosmological ideas of the present day total universe. The continued additions which are currently being made to the large body of observational knowledge may call for modifications. At the same time the field of modern cosmology may be broken down into several "schools" or attitudes. Three of them are briefly summarized in the paragraphs which follow:

(a) Suppose that stars and galaxies all had a life term. It follows that some would be of different ages than others. Fred Hoyle and his followers carried this supposition in such manner that the Universe would eventually retain its character by supposing that while some universes were in a process of decay, matter would be continuously created so that the sum total would always be preserved. The "fuel" would be the gas and dust which abounds in space and the average density of the whole would be maintained. This has been named the "Steady State"; or "Continuous Creation" Theory. Newly developed hydrogen is the building block from which the heavier elements are made by atomic interaction. Such a form of universe would have no beginning and no end.

(b) The "Explosion" Theory, suggested by the late George Gamow and others, supposes that all the material now in the Universe was originally collected in the form of a gigantic primordial fire ball. The interaction of pressure, gravity, and other forces caused it to explode; then all its component material was projected from the original center; the galaxies and stars were formed and all were endowed for a motion of spreading apart for the future. Lack of explosive debris is the principal objection to this theory.

(c) A modification of the previous theory is usually called the "Explosion-Contraction" Theory. During the expansion stage stars and galaxies are formed and are propelled into space at various speeds; during the contraction phase galaxies are slowing down and will eventually reverse their motion. The total material is finite, but time is infinite since the process is in itself one of oscillation.

Some astronomers maintain that the very application of the Doppler Principle (red shifts) to the more distant galaxies are evidence of the reasonable nature of this theory; speeds required approach that of light.

The decision as to the acceptance of one theory and rejection of others must be reserved for the future, since considerable progress in astrophysics is required. The above is necessarily simplified, since these basic theories all require a knowledge of mathematics and advanced astrophysics.

QUASARS

We have already mentioned Hubble's discovery of what is often called a law, viz:. that the velocity of recession of distant galaxies is proportioned to their distance, in other words, the greater the distance, the greater the red shift and amount of recession. It might be assumed that such a principle would pretty well take care of everything, but such is not the case. Back in 1963 we succeeded in detecting an object which, with others of its kind, has probably proven most controversial and presenting problems more difficult than any other. Quasars, short for quasi-stellar objects, are believed to be rather small in size as most giant stars go, but shine with a brilliance so great as to cause astronomers considerable astonishment. One quasar consumes an amount of energy in a year that the sun would consume during its entire stellar lifetime! The doubts expressed about these objects are shown by the wide variety of differences of interpretation. Perhaps the most startling is the suggestion that they are not really stars, but universes either in birth or death! This cannot be strictly determined because our observational material has its own limitation; but there is an additional doubt which is a critical one; Hubble's red shift principal (just mentioned above) when applied to the quasars shows there is velocity in some cases at 8/10 the velocity of light! In other words their red shift values are the largest on record!

If we are to accept our observations of the quasars as being without large error, then the astronomer is looking backward in time over 12 billion years! This immediately raises all kinds of questions regarding an expanding universe, its possible "slow down" from such a state, etc.—and all cannot be solved at present because of observational limitations. As Hamlet so well exclaimed "Aye, there's the rub!"

The above brief summary of quasars is deliberately so, partly because there is little more to add and that, highly technical. Perhaps the next generation may be able to peer a bit farther in its search for truth!

"And that inverted ball we call the Sky,
Whereunder crawling, coop'd, we live and die.
Lift not thy hand to It for help — for It
As impotently moves as you or I."

The Rubaiyat

The above words, written over 700 years ago by an astronomer poet, indicate his philosophy as derived from his lifetime wonder about the heavens and its interpretation. With our modern instruments, our ability to peer farther into space, our advancement of both astrophysics and mathematics we still look — and wonder!

Chapter IV
THE LAST WORD

The heavens provide many fascinating objects for both visual and photographic study: the Sun, Moon and planets, comets and meteors, stars and star clusters, nebulae, the Milky Way and the galaxies. All of them are a never failing source of wonder and a continued source of sustained interest which can last a lifetime. Indeed, that "inverted bowl we call the sky" has provided man with study and speculation which seems without end.

As an avocation the study of astronomy is perhaps unequalled, since it embraces so much and has such close associations, such as the fields of chemistry, physics, mathematics, philosophy, and religion. While it is true that the individual may learn much himself (and occupy the most of a lifetime in so doing), it is also true that he may learn still more from contact with others. There are many amateur astronomical societies and associations which will provide the opportunity to meet others with similar interests. As far as the contribution of valuable scientific observations may be concerned, we need only witness the work done by members of the American Association of Variable Star Observers and that of the American Meteor Society.

Much has been written in the field of astronomy, beginning even in Greek times. Many are the books and magazines in the total literature devoted to this most noble of the sciences. Perhaps it might prove rewarding for us to pause a moment and consider the progress of astronomy. There is little doubt that early man may have used the starry heavens as a means of navigation, both on water and land; very possibly he may have also used them in a form of worship; but by Greek times there arose a group of philosophers whose thinking was directed to both interpretation of what they saw and the fanciful weaving of a combination of Gods and the planets. Note that the names of many constellations go back to Greek times and even to the early civilizations in the Tigris-Euphrates Valley.

The proper explanation of the motions of the earth and its neighbors was not obtained until the time of Copernicus (1473-1543) and Kepler (1571-1630), the latter having been greatly assisted by the relatively accurate observations of Tycho Brahe (1546-1601). It was Kepler's three laws of planetary motion which placed the earth in its proper position relative to other bodies (planets). There were still no satisfactory explanations of the stars and this did not come until the invention of the telescope by Galileo (1564-1642) and the improvements in its usefulness by others; however, the true understanding of the stars as suns like our own and the structure and motion of our galaxy were products of recent centuries. As a striking contrast we may remark that the observers of the Mayan civilization (Mexico and Central America) obtained a value of the length of the year of considerable accuracy in Roman times—and this without instruments! We know relatively little about these people, but we do know that their knowledge of the motion of the planet Venus was determined with an exceedingly high accuracy.

One of the factors which held back astronomical advancement had always been a lack of knowledge of mechanics (physics); this was supplied by Isaac Newton (1642-1747) and his followers. His laws of motion and the mutual reactions of any two bodies are really the corner stone of modern astronomy, since they deliniate our solar system.

A hundred years ago physical scientists were certain that all processes of the physical world could be handled with increasingly greater degrees of accuracy in measurement and that the setting of the position and velocity of a particle in a Newtonian system guaranteed its position for any time in the past and in the future.

This beautiful concept was destroyed by the coming of modern physics (atomic) and the pronouncements of Albert Einstein. Now it seems that mass and energy are interchangeable, that location in time as well as location in space must be considered, and that the determination of the structure of the total universe is not a matter of a few hours of calculation.

Einstein's Relativity Theory has revolutionized our thinking concerning space, time, mass and energy and it is of the utmost importance in many of the calculations and interpretations of modern astronomy. In addition, the application of Hubble's Law remains a subject of considerable question.

Many beginners may ask, "Is it possible for me to learn all this!" The answer is that an abundant and inexhaustible fund of patience coupled with a will to learn will eventually bring success. For a good parallel read the life of Galileo or that of Isaac Newton. It is true that not all beginners are going to be Galileos or Newtons, but all may obtain the basic knowledge and concepts which are so necessary to an understanding of "what it is all about". Throughout a lifetime such learning will produce much personal satisfaction.

Much can be learned by word of mouth; still more, perhaps, from the printed page; but the great treasure chest of the starry heavens is forever filled with wonders and lessons. Continued and patient study gives one the key which unlocks these treasures.

"The world, the race, the soul—in space and time the universes,
All bound as is befitting each—all surely going somewhere."

Walt Whitman

APPENDIX

OPTICAL AIDS

Many observers are not completely satisfied with the limitations of the naked eye for observation and wish some directions regarding the instruments provided by modern science. Needless to say, there are many such instruments and a brief discussion of them will at least serve as a point of departure.

The first and perhaps the best instrument to be used by the beginner is the common field glass, designed so that two optical barrels are operated simultaneously and thus give some magnification compared with the eyes alone. This instrument is classed as 4x, 6x, or 8x to indicate the amount of optical power as compared with the eye, the 8x being slightly more powerful and therefore slightly more useful. The instrument is focused by manipulation of a knurled knob which causes the barrels to be properly adjusted so as to accommodate the requirements of the eyes; the more modern types provide for the focus of each eye independently.

There is no question that the field glasses (or binoculars) are fairly easy to handle and quite portable. One is even tempted to purchase 10x or 12x, but we must remember that larger and heavier instruments become awkward to hold and manipulate. Furthermore, we must realize that they may require some sort of bracket or tripod to hold the instrument steady while observing; in addition we find (perhaps to our surprise) that the turbulence in the earth's atmosphere becomes more pronounced at the same rate as the object to be seen. This is annoying, but is difficult to overcome, especially in areas of polluted air. The best "seeing" is to be found in rural localities.

Consider a pair of field glasses, but confine your attention to only one of the two elements as though we were making use of a single eye. We will find that we have an instrument consisting of two parts: (1) The larger lens, whose main purpose is to gather the light of an object (the moon, a star or a distant mountain peak); (2) a magnifying lens (the part where the eye is placed) whose sole purpose is to enlarge the image obtained from the gathered light. This arrangement is equally true of the type of telescope invented by Galileo and containing a light gathering lens about two inches in diameter, mounted at one end of a piece of tubing, plus a small adjustable eyepiece. Such a telescope is called a refracting type because the light passes through the lens system. In practice the lenses are not of the simple convex type, but are compound (a pair of lenses fitting together). The light gatherer is called the objective and may range in diameter from a few inches to as much as 36 or 40 inches. The magnifier is small and is adjustable in distance by the use of a knurled knob operating on a traveling track; it is properly called the eyepiece; however, the telescope is designed for ease with one eye instead of the twin arrangement of the field glasses. Galileo's telescope had a magnifying power of 32 (as compared with the unaided eye). Some of todays small refractors may use 60 to 200 powers.

There are certain practical limits to the construction and use of a refracting telescope. In its place we may use the type invented by Isaac Newton and called the reflector, since it employs a mirror in place of the objective lens. Such a mirror is mounted at one end of a tube so that the light travels down the tube, is reflected back and then employs one of several devices to be properly magnified by an eyepiece as before.

There are several reasons why most large telescopes designed and built today are reflectors, viz. (1) a mirror having but one surface is much easier constructed than the four faces of a compound lens; (2) the mirror's surface reflects the light and there is no great loss of light by absorption when passing through the compound lens; (3) in general a reflector is shorter in length than a refractor of equal light gathering power; (4) the engineering problems of supporting a large reflector are easier than an equal refractor.

The instrument commonly used by astronomers (professional or amateur) is the telescope. It is more powerful, sometime portable, more often fixed in location, and may be very expensive. The reader is referred to the many existing books on the subject. They may be purchased or they may be found in the larger public libraries. The purchase of a good telescope should not be made until a thorough background of knowledge is obtained. Remember that a good telescope is not cheap! They range in price from about $250 to as much as $1500. An investment of such magnitude should be considered carefully! There is a saying that "you get what you pay for"; it is indeed true here, as a telescope which is cheap in price will be a cheap telescope in its performance. The area of optical instruments is one in which there is no compromise with good quality! As a rough guide a 2½ inch refractor, with mounting, costs about $150, while a 6 inch reflector is in the $200 and $300 class. The greater light gathering power of the latter is well worth while. Note that the eyepiece used depends upon the "seeing conditions", which will vary widely, even in a selected location.

The above is a bare outline. It must be supplemented by further study; incidentally, some telescopes are available in "build-it-yourself" kits.

REFERENCES

The publications in the field of astronomy are now so large in number and the material is changing so rapidly, so that the beginner had best be advised to apply to his city or county library and look under the appropriate Dewey Classification number for the available books. However, it may be best to restrict one's selections to those books of recent issue—certainly not earlier than 1960. New books are appearing constantly and cover all such sub-divisions as moon exploration, the Universe, the galaxy, the solar system, the amateur astronomer, the telescope, theories of stellar energy and behavior, amateur photography, comets and meteors, etc.

In addition the following publications are of value and within the comprehension of the beginner:

Natural History, 10 issues. $8.00, Central Park West at 7th St., New York, 10024.

Sky and Telescope, 12 issues. $9.00, 49 Bay State Rd., Cambridge, Mass., 02139.

Either or both are sometimes available in the local library.

INDEX